GOOD · OLD · DAYS®

City
SIDEWALKS
in the GOOD OLD DAYS™

Edited by Ken & Janice Tate

City Sidewalks in the Good Old Days™

Editors: Ken and Janice Tate
Managing Editor: Barb Sprunger
Editorial Assistant: Sara Meyer
Copy Supervisor: Michelle Beck
Copy Editors: Mary O'Donnell, Läna Schurb

Publishing Services Director: Brenda Gallmeyer
Art Director: Brad Snow
Assistant Art Director: Nick Pierce
Graphic Arts Supervisor: Ronda Bechinski
Production Artists: Nicole Gage, Janice Tate
Production Assistants: Marj Morgan, Judy Neuenschwander
Photography Supervisor: Tammy Christian
Photography: Matthew Owen
Photo Stylist: Tammy Steiner

Printed in China
First Printing: 2010
Library of Congress Number: 2009928697
ISBN: 978-1-59217-269-6

Good Old Days Customer Service: (800) 829-5865

Every effort has been made to ensure the accuracy of the material in this book.
However, the publisher is not responsible for research errors or typographical mistakes in this publication.

We would like to thank the following for the art prints used in this book.
For fine-art prints and more information on the artists featured in *City Sidewalks in the Good Old Days* contact:
Curtis Publishing, Indianapolis, IN 46202, (317) 633-2070, All rights reserved, www.curtispublishing.com
Applejack Art Partners, Manchester Center, VT 05255 (802) 362-3662, www.applejackart.com

DRGbooks.com

1 2 3 4 5 6 7 8 9

Dear Friends of the Good Old Days,

Most of the readers of *Good Old Days* magazine from the two decades that I have served as editor would assume that I am pretty much a country boy—and I am.

Raised in the hill country of the Ozark Mountains of southern Missouri, my toes wiggled in dirt from the time I was born until I was in my mid-20s. But that doesn't mean that I never knew what life along city sidewalks was like.

One of my favorite city memories from my youth is when a Boy Scout troop was started in a nearby town when I was about 10 or 11. My father served as Scoutmaster, and his son simply had to have a Scout uniform.

In those days there was no place to buy a uniform locally, and if there was a way to order one my folks didn't know about it. The closest store that handled Scout uniforms was Barth's Clothing Store in the bustling metropolis of Springfield, 60 miles away.

That distance was a huge trip to a youngster who had hardly been out of the county in which he had been born. Today the trip between Branson and Springfield is on U.S. 65, a four-lane freeway that carries thousands of cars each day. Back then U.S. 65 was a twisting country road that today is known as State Highway 248. It was sparsely travelled and connected several hamlets to the largest city in the southern part of the state. To me, that blacktop ribbon was as good as any magic carpet ride.

And if the drive was an adventure, Springfield itself was a revelation!

Never before had I seen so many cars, so many buildings and so many people. That was amplified all the more as we approached the Public Square.

On the Square was the movie theater, the Heer's ("since 1879") Building, the 10-story Missouri State office building, and Woolworth's and Barth's (pictured below in a postcard from the 1940s). I know there were several other landmarks there, but those are the ones that stand out in my memory.

Barth's was a two-story building near the northwest corner of the Square. After securing my uniform (only the shirt part because that was all my parents could afford), we spent the rest of that glorious Saturday exploring the urban landscape.

When we returned home, my life was simply transformed. I had heard my own version of that old song from World War I: "How ya gonna keep him down on the farm after he's seen Springfield?"

When I married a country girl who had likewise led a sheltered life, we decided to travel a different road than our parents had. The ensuing years took us to Los Angeles, Dallas and a few other city sidewalks we called home. Though we returned to our hills much later in life, we have had our fair share of good memories from those urban days.

Likewise, this book is filled with so many good memories of city life contributed by our readers through the years. Janice and I hope you enjoy this stroll down those City Sidewalks in the Good Old Days.

⊰ Contents ⊱

On the Block • 6

That's Entertainment! • 34

The Beat of the Street • 66

Getting Around Town • 100

East Side, West Side • 124

On the Block

Chapter One

Fun was where you could find it back in the Good Old Days. In my young mind, there was no more fun place to visit than my Uncle Harley's and Aunt Nellie's home in Kansas City.

Fun happened whenever my big brother, baby sister and I were able to be around any of our cousins, but Dale, Tim and Rick were particularly fun experts because they lived in the city, whereas almost all the rest of our dozens of cousins lived in the country.

Back home, I never knew what it meant to have neighborhood friends. Our closest neighbors were Grandma Stamps and Aunt Martha, both elderly widows and both about a quarter-mile away. The nearest family with children around our ages was about two miles down the country road.

But at Uncle Harley's home, there were kids right there on the block! We teamed up with our cousins and played baseball against the neighbors on the vacant lot nearby. We played King of the Hill, Hide and Seek and a myriad of other games. If you've ever tried to play King of the Hill with a big brother five years your senior and a little sister two years your junior, you can understand why the presence of all those youngsters was a thrill to me.

On the block with its sidewalks we could roller-skate and ride scooters with our cousins and their buddies. Sister Donna learned how to play hopscotch with the neighborhood girls. Brother Dennis, already in his teenage years, found more mature things to do, like talk with girls while lounging on Uncle Harley's lawn.

The grown-ups would spend their time drinking lemonade and talking in the cool of the front porch. Sometimes they pulled out mallets and wickets to play a rousing game of croquet. They wouldn't let us youngsters play, mainly because we turned the game into a type of lawn polo, galloping like we were on horseback and slapping the balls toward the wickets as if they were tiny goals.

It was several years later that I discovered the genteel nature of the game. It was a favorite amongst neighbors who liked to play a sport that required less sweat and more strategy. Still, it never seemed neighborly to me when a player placed his foot on his croquet ball next to one controlled by the opposition (see the 1951 *Saturday Evening Post* painting at left), and then slapped his ball with the mallet. The move always knocked the opposing ball halfway across the lawn and out of contention.

Life on the block was a great place to be a kid. I discovered that on summer days at Uncle Harley's. The stories in this chapter will take you back to those days when sidewalks in the city were mostly safe for children. They will illustrate a time when latchkey kids were unheard of. And they will remind us of when "Love thy neighbor" was more than a commandment. It was something we all learned and did every day while we were living On the Block.

—*Ken Tate*

> *They usually wouldn't let us youngsters play, mainly because we turned the game into a type of lawn polo.*

When Fire Hydrants Were Red

By Ginger K. Nelson

During the 1940s, in a borough called Wood-Ridge, N.J. (a suburb of the sprawling New York City), young people enjoyed wholesome activities that didn't cost much money. It was a simpler time; you didn't dare say you had nothing to do, or someone—a parent, relative or neighbor—would find something unpleasant that needed to be done. So we always found our own entertainment. Life wasn't complicated back when fire hydrants were red.

I remember a hopscotch grid drawn with white chalk on the concrete sidewalk, and a piece of tar for a marker. I remember playing Mother, May I?; Red Light, Green Light; Hide-and-Seek; Giant Step; and Statue on the rarely traveled streets. Cowboys (and cowgirls) and Indians gave vent to our politically incorrect imaginations. Evenings after supper, neighborhood kids gathered to play these and other games, back when fire hydrants were red.

> *Climbing trees and screaming at the top of our lungs was quite freeing to our restless souls.*

There was an area across from my house that we called "the woods." It contained trees and trails and somebody's crudely built tree house. We used to crawl up to the platform, using handholds on the bark, and pretend that the flimsy structure was our house or fort. Climbing trees and screaming at the top of our lungs in that deserted area, where there were no neighbors to complain and no parents to holler at us, was quite freeing to our restless souls. We gathered tiny berries from bushes and mashed them into magical paint. Nature fostered our imagination, back when fire hydrants were red.

There were abandoned railroad tracks on which we could balance at the dead end of every street. There were concrete sidewalks that were built in squares that got upended and led to frequently skinned knees.

We especially enjoyed the deli, where we could sometimes get free pickles while sniffing the garlicky sandwich meats and salads. And there was the bakery, where the staff allowed us to peek at the sugary sweets behind the counter and play "What would you choose if you could have just one thing?" These were some of the places we flocked to, back when fire hydrants were red.

Parties held the promise of Pin the Tail on the Donkey, scavenger hunts and somebody's mother's homemade chocolate cake. Little girls wore gingham hand-me-down dresses with new Mary Jane shoes, and they never invited boys to their birthday celebrations. These were treasured times, back when fire hydrants were red.

Riding bikes or clamp roller skates made chestnut picking an exciting event. We carved the chestnuts into bubble pipes that never worked. The lots where we found them were abundant, and everything there was free and safe. On rainy days, girls would drip colored candles into circles on waxed paper. When they were cool, we strung the wax circles onto necklaces and bracelets, and sold a few in the neighborhood.

Another popular activity was painting shells we had found on beach outings. They became colorful decorations our parents always loved. We always found something to make, back when fire hydrants were red.

Once we were older, we reveled in pin-your-hair-up slumber parties with other pre-teens who wore long, flowered, flannel pajamas and hairnets. Charades and Scrabble fueled our competitive fires. Shooting each other with plastic water guns and playing ghost with our mothers' all-white mended sheets kept us busy. (Sheets were never floral or plaid or striped in the days when fire hydrants were red.)

Halloween was our favorite holiday because of the treats we accumulated in our pillowcases, but the night before Halloween, *aka* "Mischief Night" or "Cabbage Night" was even more fun when we reached the upper grammar school grades. We considered it acceptable to play harmless pranks. We penned threatening notes, writing things like "The ghost is going to get you!" in our childish scrawls, and left them in unlocked cars.

There was also a piece of porous graphite that sounded like breaking glass when it was rubbed on windows. After performing our

A photo of the author in 1945 with her favorite toys.

mischief on a house's windows, we would hide in bushes to watch the reactions. It sure made unsuspecting people angry!

Once we tried this on someone who had a sick child. He came outside to give us the dickens, which we deserved. That was the end of our graphite-grinding, although we sure liked to "frighten" people with innocent pranks, back when fire hydrants were red.

High school days held many memories, but the prom, when we wore carnations on our net-and-tulle gowns, was extra special. At our parochial school, we always had to visit the convent to show our dresses to the nuns before going to the dance, who made sure that our gowns were appropriately modest. They always seemed to have cloaks at the ready for the girls who dared to wear strapless concoctions. We also enjoyed Sadie Hawkins dances, where the boys wore vegetable corsages, back when fire hydrants were red.

It was also a time for donning black-and-white saddle shoes or white bucks. Neon-colored socks often accompanied them, making the shoes seem to glow. Maybe it was just a fad where I lived, but a dog collar on an ankle showed a girl's eligibility, depending on the ankle on which it was worn. At the five and dime we could buy sturdy chains for displaying our boyfriends' class rings. High school letters from school athletes which were sewn on sweaters also made our preferences known. We thought we were "george," back when fire hydrants were red.

I'm sure other people have different memories, depending on where they lived, but this suburban girl remembers commonplace games, unusual fads and innocent fun from her time in the Good Old Days, when fire hydrants were red. ❖

In the Middle of the Block

By Alma Quinlan

Sitting in the middle of the block in the middle of Queens, N.Y., the house stood three stories tall. It seemed totally unsuited to the tree-lined neighborhood of old Cape Cods; built more like a barn, it would have been well suited to a farm. It was called the Jockey's Hotel, and aptly so, since the jockeys from nearby Aqueduct Racetrack lived there.

It is not certain when the jockeys abandoned the beautiful house to live elsewhere, but what *is* certain is that my grandfather, John DiNardi, purchased it from the Pizzo family to keep his family together in the late 1930s.

John and Lucia DiNardi had six children, all single adults when they moved into that unforgettable house. It was a myriad of rooms, some small and some big, with three bathrooms, three large garages, a courtyard and a moderately sized backyard.

It was the first home in which my sister, brother and I lived, and it is the house to which we attach the fondest memories. Three floors of family! No matter where we went in that house, we were sure to run into grandparents, aunts and uncles, and we were sure to get hugs and kisses at every turn. Aunts and uncles taught us to play boxball, pick-up sticks and jump rope—simple activities for a much simpler time. Wrapped in the security of a loving family, we hoped that nothing would ever change.

The author's parents on the stoop of the house in Queens, 1941.

Every floor had wonderful smells of food cooking—mouthwatering tomato sauce, dripping with olive oil, surrounding meatballs and sausages, roasts, soups and peppers. And always, loaves of Italian bread at every meal.

My brother rode his big three-wheeler, and my sister and I rolled our doll carriages up and down that flat, straight sidewalk under the watchful eyes of parents and relatives.

On holidays, everyone gathered around the delicious Old World cuisine, visiting in a constant chatter in both English and Italian.

Seasoning the mix was the laughter of my grandmother, who totally enjoyed everyone and everything.

Later, after the meal had ended, and after the anisette, coffee and Italian pastries had been served, my mother would play the piano and everyone would sing. The older relatives once again exchanged stories about the Old Country, reminiscing, crying and finally rejoicing in being with family to enjoy the holiday. If I close my eyes, I am there again, smelling the cooking and hearing the voices of relatives gone to God.

My brother, sister and I dreamed of getting married, buying that house and again filling it with children, cooking and love. We did marry and have children, but we never followed through on that part of our dream—to live in that wonderful house in the middle of the block, in the middle of Queens. ❖

BILLS
BIRD
HOUSE
SHOP

U.S. MAIL

JOHN FALTER

From the Porch Swing

By Don C. Miller

The Southern environment that was my world as a child was more than a geographical location in central Florida. It was a way of life defined by my maternal grandmother, Ida Mae Grubbs, and viewed from the weathered swing on our front porch.

Many early memories of my grandmother and our life in Ocala revolved around this porch swing. Our front porch spanned the entire width of our frame house. The wooden porch floor creaked to the step, and gray paint peeled from its surface. Clay pots of geraniums with exquisite red blossoms and velvety green leaves lined the porch railings next to the swing.

Other flowers bordered the porch in an array of equally brilliant colors because of my grandmother's dedication to making our small corner of the world a little brighter through flowers. Hollyhocks rose majestically in front of the railing, their rows of towering pink blossoms reaching for the Florida sky.

Lilies grew by the side of the porch and bloomed before Easter. They heralded the coming of spring and the promise of the renewal it always brings. The lilies' fragile white blossoms were silhouetted against the purplish hues of the sturdier neighboring hydrangeas.

Our home's convenient corner location was two blocks from downtown. It was a frequent stopping point for friends and neighbors who passed by on their way to town. Visits with my grandmother, who was loved for her spirit and Southern witticisms, brightened everyone's day. She welcomed everyone to enjoy a brief respite on our porch swing so they would not be "all tuckered out" from their walk to town. I still remember the rhythmic sounds of the swing and my grandmother's delightful laughter as visitors swung back and forth while sharing memories and news.

Others less fortunate stopped by for a free meal at my grandmother's ample table. My grandmother was a firm believer in the Golden Rule, and she practiced it whenever she had the opportunity. During the late 1930s and early 1940s, it was not unusual for someone who was "down on his luck" to stop by our home; many people who were out of work came to the South. My grandmother always saw to it that those who stopped at our house received a nourishing meal of steaming fresh vegetables, corn bread and a refreshing glass of tea.

Our home was a frequent stopping point for friends and neighbors who passed by on their way to town.

Although these people often offered to work for their food, my grandmother did not require them to do so. She simply served her delicious Southern fare to these unexpected visitors with a smile and a kind word. And somehow, she always managed to have enough to share in spite of our very limited resources.

These itinerants usually sat on the porch steps in the shade of the oleander tree as they ate. They enthralled all of us children with stories about the dreams that had brought them to the South. My grandmother's blue eyes were often clouded by tears when these strangers left. She wondered where they would get their next meal—or another kind word.

My grandmother taught me a lot about life in the years she lived with us. Through her example, I learned what it means to survive adversity and yet maintain hope by going through life with an unconquerable spirit. From my perch on our porch swing, I also learned what it means to share true Southern hospitality with all who come our way. It is a legacy I still cherish. ❖

A Good Place

By Ardene Monte

Today, I often tell people that I grew up in a good place at a good time, had a lot of fun and never got into any trouble. The "good place" was LaSalle, Peru and Oglesby, three cities on the Illinois River, about 100 miles southwest of Chicago. That was in the 1930s. My name back then was Ardene Monterastelli, and I was one happy kid.

Our whole life revolved around sports back then—baseball, whenever we could find a place to play (usually the street, an alley or a vacant lot), and basketball in the winter.

We would shovel the snow away and put up a basket on the garage. We played football too, wherever there was room.

We couldn't wait to get home after school, change our clothes and go out to play. Mother would call us for supper. We didn't respond right away, but when Dad called, we couldn't get in the door fast enough. We never said "Later on!" or "In a little while!" to him. Dad didn't know those words—but he knew where the razor strop hung in the bathroom!

One time we were playing baseball on one of the diamonds at Hegler Park and some big kids ran us off. "You guys aren't so hot!" we yelled. "How about playing us? We haven't won a game yet, but we haven't lost a fight, either!"

Oh, we got into a lot of fights, all right. One day, Geno Pierro and I got into an argument at school. We decided to meet in an alley after school for a fight. I don't remember what Geno got, but I know I went home with a bloody nose. From then on, Geno was my best friend.

Then came high school, and I became a teenager. I soon discovered dancing and girls— or I should say, girls and dancing. We had two great places to dance—the auditorium in LaSalle, and Starved Rock State Park in the summertime.

The auditorium had a new-car showroom on the first floor (usually only one car—a Buick, I think); the second floor was a big dance hall. My buddies had been dancing awhile, so they were all good dancers. There were no dance classes or lessons in those days—everybody just had their own style. Once they got me started dancing, I couldn't get enough of it.

We always got the Big Bands from the Trianon and Aragon in Chicago, so the music was great. Some of us worked as ushers at the local theaters—the Majestic and the LaSalle Theater. On Saturdays we would meet after work at Duffy's Cigar Store downtown, pool our money, and head off to the dance.

> *We always got the Big Bands from the Trianon and Aragon in Chicago, so the music was great.*

The other great place to dance was the pavilion at Starved Rock. It was a big dance hall with wooden sides that opened and folded down outside. Tables and chairs surrounded the floor.

Before we went to the dances, we always picked up Bob Shields. His parents owned the funeral home in Oglesby, and we would take leftover flowers to the girls. They thought we were great, and we certainly made a lot of points with them.

I graduated from high school in 1938. I was going to Illinois Wesleyan when Pearl Harbor was attacked. In 1942, I graduated, moved to Los Angeles, and went to work at Northrop Aircraft for the duration of the war.

I retired in 1987 and moved to Palm Springs, Calif., enjoying the good life—sunshine, working and playing on the golf courses. In 2004, I moved to Smyrna, Ga. I am living in DelMar Gardens, an independent living facility.

They're all nice places to live, of course, but none of them is as good as the "good place" of my youth. ❖

Windy City Memories

By Dorothy Anna Birkholz

Looking back to the days when I was a child, I'm amazed to think how differently children played then. We did not have the toys and games children have today, but we were happy, fun loving and imaginative.

I was born in Chicago and lived there for 40 years. I remember playing store with the three sisters who lived next door. It took some time before we could start because we had to hunt for our "products" first.

The author (far right) is shown with neighborhood friends (left to right) Edwin, Ella and Julia May (with doll).

We gathered large stones to use for potatoes, smaller stones for eggs and sand for sugar. We pulled up dandelions for carrots and gathered weeds for spinach. One tree had long pods filled with seeds; we gathered them and used them for beans. We tore old newspaper into squares, folded the squares into cones and used these for bags. We tore paper into pieces to use for our money. Thus equipped, we played store for hours.

We also enjoyed jumping rope. We all had pieces of our mothers' old clotheslines; no "boughten" jump ropes for us.

My favorite jumping game was Double Dutch, played by turning two ropes in the opposite directions at the same time.

We all liked to play jacks. In those days, we could get a ball and jacks for 10 cents.

We were all lucky enough to own roller skates. Mine were handed down from my sister, who was 12 years older than I was. The heavy metal skates clamped onto our shoes and were tightened in place with a key.

I mustn't forget hopscotch. We drew numbered squares on the sidewalk with chalk and used a piece of glass or a little flat stone for a "lager" to throw.

Evenings in the summer, our parents would sit out on the front porch, and we played a game we made up. Three of us sat on the bottom step and the fourth girl held a stone in one fist. She held out both closed hands and one girl would tap the hand she thought held the stone. If she guessed right, she moved up a step. Each one got a turn, and whoever got to the top step and back down first was the winner. The one with the stone put her hands behind her each time; we never knew if she'd changed it, or if the stone was still in the same hand.

We also enjoyed playing Hide-and-Seek; Tag; London Bridge; and Run, Sheep, Run. Of course, we always had stories and jokes to tell. Some stories were real and some were made up.

Kids today probably would laugh about our games, but we were truly happy and were good friends.

Those three "girls" still live in Chicago, and we keep in touch with letters and phone calls. We still remember our good times in the Good Old Days. ❖

Wheels on Our Feet

By Robert A. Halligan

When talking about the Good Old Days, most people think about life on a farm or in a small town. I grew up in the middle of New York City in a tenement. We lived on the top floor of a four-story walk-up, and for a little boy, those three flights of stairs were not much different from the Alps. In the early 1920s, New York already was a city of concrete.

Central Park was too far away for our short legs, so we played in the streets. Tossing a rubber ball around was the best we could do at first, but as we acquired skill, we advanced to punchball and later to stickball. The latter was baseball played with a rubber ball, a broomstick bat and improvised bases.

Neighbors didn't like it because of broken windows, although, to be honest, they were surprisingly rare.

Bicycles were a far-off dream, so we rode tricycles and pedal cars, but it was a chore to haul them up from basements. Roller skates became the wheels of choice, and everybody had a pair. The sidewalks were slabs of stone and too rough for skating, so we skated in the street.

Immediately, I can hear screams of horror from parents at the idea of little boys skating in the streets of New York. But I can assure you that cars were few and far between at the time, and it was quite safe. The street's surface was smooth and level; nothing could be sweeter for skaters.

We learned to skate at an early age and quickly became proficient. When a new learner appeared, we rallied 'round to help him acquire skill. Skaters today wear helmets and lots of padding, but we never gave that a thought. I can't recall anybody suffering more than a minor scrape or bruise.

Like men comparing the merits of cars, we discussed makes of skates. Far and away the most popular was Union Hardware, with Winslow a poor second. When Union Hardware wheels wore out, they could "run on the rims" for a while, whereas Winslow wheels lost their bearings and had to be replaced at once. And Winslow wheels were hard to find, while Union Hardware wheels were available in many toy stores and hardware stores.

The most memorable thing about skating was the disappearing

skate key. Skate keys were stamped from cheap sheet metal, and one key accompanied every new pair of skates. That key was indispensable because it was needed to adjust toe clamps or skate length, or to replace a wheel. Those skate keys were important, and so one might suppose that they were zealously guarded. Still, it was miraculous the way those keys disappeared, and I am at a loss to explain it. They could be threaded onto the ankle straps, but nobody bothered because it was too much trouble to unfasten and refasten the strap when a key was needed. After all, we were just kids. But the fellow who always had a key in his pocket enjoyed much popularity.

There were two problems with skates: The ankle straps became painful when they dug into the flesh too long, and the toe clamps, even though they were adjustable, wouldn't hold unless the sole of the skater's shoe was

1956 *Wee Wisdom* cover from the collection of Janice Tate

very stiff. Thus we couldn't skate while wearing sneakers. Sheepskin pads solved the strap problem, but it wasn't until years later that the clamps were replaced with "wings" that covered the toes. Then we could wear sneakers or even bedroom slippers!

In winter, the Central Park lake sometimes froze over and was open for skating, but we didn't go very often because of the distance, and because few of us had ice skates. Also, watching our shoes was a problem. Roller skating was our chief sport from pre-school to high school.

When I was 10, my family moved across the bridge to Queens, part of New York City. It was a corner house, and it so happened that the corner was the gathering place for many neighborhood boys who were about my age, so I fit right in. The kids came from two schools: Public School 63, a block and a half away, and Nativity, two blocks away. The streets were only half-paved, so we couldn't skate, but the sidewalks were concrete and not too bad for skating. As we grew older, bicycles became fairly common, but we quickly realized that bicycles didn't lend themselves to games like skates did. As few as three skaters could at least play tag.

For a while, we did most of our skating on Public School 63's concrete playground—until they put up a fence and locked us out. No doubt the city feared a lawsuit in case of an injury.

At about that time, Liberty Avenue, one block north, was paved over. For a while it became our skating rink, until it was completed to City Line and traffic became too much for us. Then the city fathers paved the avenue in front

Harold, Robert and Donald Halligan (left to right) in 1928 face 107th Avenue, where most of the roller-skating took place.

of our house. That solved our skating problem for years, because it was a side street and there never was much traffic.

We used calcimine to paint a goal around a sewer cover and another goal a couple of covers away, making a fine hockey rink. Every winter there were games. For pucks, we used wooden disks about an inch thick, but they were too light and tended to roll. To add weight and discourage rolling, we bored a hole in the middle and filled it with molten lead. If there was an odd man out, he became the referee; otherwise, we tried to play with a minimum of argument.

For years the skaters were all boys, but when we reached our teens, the fairer sex joined us, one or two at a time. A few even played hockey. Romances started to blossom. Most evenings there were skaters of both sexes on the avenue, leading to impromptu skating parties, and hockey games were seen less and less.

All good things must end, and skating was no exception, but it didn't happen all at once. Probably the biggest factor was high school, with its late-afternoon hours and much more homework than grammar school. But it was odd that the younger kids didn't take our place and keep things going. Perhaps the cars scared them, although traffic on the avenue never was heavy.

We were growing up. We were dating. We were going to home parties, school dances and sports events. I guess it was only natural that spin the bottle should replace roller skating, but either way, they were the Good Old Days. ❖

Marshmallows and Hot Dogs

By Susan Ahlswede

lick, clack, clickety-clack … Our roller skates hummed along the best skating sidewalk in the neighborhood. Back in the 1940s, not everyone was fortunate enough to have a concrete or asphalt driveway. So before we fastened our metal roller skates to our shoes, tightening them with keys, we always swept the stones and cinders back into the two driveways along the sidewalk to avoid hitting one and falling head over heels.

Then, starting at the mailbox on the corner by Mrs. Laminsky's house, we would have smooth sailing, past Piette's well-kept yellow and brown house, and past our own large, two-story, gray stucco home, until we were about three sidewalk squares past our driveway. Then we had to maneuver around or jump over a couple of cracked squares by Mr. Estey's house. After that, we skated smoothly again down to the corner.

Pleasant memories drift back when I think about my childhood in the 1940s–1950s in Appleton, Wis. Mr. Estey, a slight, white-haired gentleman, will always be part of those memories. His two-story white house was surrounded by huge maples and elms that produced an abundance of beautiful autumn leaves.

Photograph © 2009 by Maxime Perron Caissy and www.sxc.hu

The neighborhood kids, including my younger sister, Barbara, and me, loved to rake leaves for him. We'd all bring our rakes over to his yard on a cool, crisp October afternoon and rake the leaves into huge mounds. Then we'd take flying leaps and sink into the middle of a just-raked pile. I can still feel the soft, crackling landing. We would come up with dry, powdery leaves in our hair, clothes and mouths—and we loved every minute of it!

After we'd had our fun, we'd rake the leaves back into a neat pile and wait for the invitation. We crossed our fingers and hoped Mr. Estey would ask if we wanted to have a hot dog–and–marshmallow roast, burning the leaves in his outdoor fireplace. We were thrilled when he asked us to come back at 8 o'clock that night to enjoy the special treat. He usually supplied the hot dogs and marshmallows.

My sister, our friends and I would gather around the glowing orange flames and enjoy their wonderfully pungent aroma as we reminisced about our fun-filled week. I don't remember everything we talked about on those special nights, but I do remember the warmth we felt for each other and how important Mr. Estey made us feel. I think we could use more Mr. Esteys today! ❖

The Stoop

By Marty Toohey

The word "stoop" probably originated in the Bronx, where apartment buildings outnumbered private homes by a wide margin. During the 1930s, stoops were indispensable. Stoops served as the stairway entrances to most apartment buildings. Tenants sat on the stone steps of their building's stoop during spring and summer. And every kid in the neighborhood knew that without a stoop, there would be no stoopball games.

The stoop was also a specific location. "I'll meet you on your stoop at 6 o'clock," he might have said. Thus there was no question about where they would meet; she had only one stoop, and it never moved.

"I just saw him playing on the stoop a moment ago. He's here somewhere." Whoever they were looking for was close by.

Children play on a door stoop in Georgetown, Washington, D.C., in 1935. Photo courtesy of the Library of Congress.

"Let's go down and sit on the stoop. It's like a furnace up here." It was always cooler on the stoop in the summer.

"Aunt Kitty just got home. I saw her going up the stoop." Aunt Kitty was definitely home by now.

"I want all you kids off this stoop!" This was a daily challenge from the building janitor to a group of noisy kids.

"Bring a cushion down from the kitchen. There's room on the stoop." A cushion provided the ultimate luxury when sitting on a concrete stoop.

"Move off the stoop. Let me through!" Mrs. McKenna was returning with bundles. "Carry my groceries up the stoop, Sonny. I'll give you a few pennies for yourself."

"Wanna play stoopball?" If the stoop wasn't occupied by sitters, a Spaldeen properly aimed at the edge of a stoop step could rebound clear across the street and score a point in a stoopball game.

Not every apartment building in the neighborhood had a stoop. Some building entrances were level with the sidewalk. And some stoops had only one or two steps.

The stoop at 1195 Boston Road had six steps. When I was real small, a Western Union telegram man rushed past me as I sat on our stoop. His black leather leggings whizzed by as he jumped three steps at a time. Three steps at a time! I had never seen that before.

As I grew taller, I learned to scale the stoop two steps at a time and then, later, three. From that day forward, I always climbed the stairs of a stoop at least two steps at a time—and when descending, I always "leaped," as we called it, from the top step of a stoop to the sidewalk.

Vinnie Comiskey lived at 1123 Fulton Avenue, next to the German church. He was in our sixth-grade class at St. Augustine's until he moved. We played with Vinnie and his sister Caramel. (Carrie's real name was "Carmel," but we called her "Caramel," like the candy.)

James Tofaro's parents were the janitors at 1123. Mr. Tofaro made Mrs. Tofaro do most of the work scrubbing the hallway stairs.

The stoop at 1123 was flanked by a swooping stone structure on each side. It made for a neat sliding pond if Mr. Tofaro wasn't sitting there. We would scramble up the six stoop steps on roller skates, twist and jump onto the top of the swoop, stand up quickly and then rocket all the way down to the sidewalk. It was a distance of no more than 6 feet, but it felt like 60.

Vinnie's stoop was also handy for playing stoopball if Jackie's stoop at 1121 was too crowded. And its sliding ponds enabled us to compete to see who could bounce a Spaldeen across the street the farthest.

Mrs. Bannon lived on the second floor in Aunt Kitty's apartment house at 1121 Fulton. Whenever Mrs. Bannon wanted to come downstairs and sit on the stoop, Aunt Kitty had to help her down and sit with her, then help her back up, because she had a wooden leg.

One day I was sitting on the stoop with my friends, telling stories and joking. Everyone laughed when I imitated how Mrs. Bannon went up and down the stairs with her wooden leg—and how one time I even saw the wooden part. I got a lot of laughs from the other kids, but one of them told on me. Aunt Kitty scolded me and made me apologize to Mrs. Bannon. Then my mother scolded me because she was a friend of Mrs. Bannon's. But I still thought it was funny.

Many years later, when I was married with kids, I lived in various houses with porches, patios, decks and terraces. I never heard anyone say "I'll meet you on the patio at 6 o'clock" or "Let's play deck ball."

How you gonna play stoopball if you don't have a stoop? ❖

The Skate Key

By Betty Kossick

There's a key that hangs on a special little hook in my house. The heart-shaped hook holds a skate key—and it evokes nostalgic memories. However, this particular key was not mine. This key was a gift from a dear friend, Sharon.

She found it hidden under a porch banister in the home she rented in Pasadena, Calif., in 1980. She recalled the scar on my left knee. I'd explained that it was a result of frequent falls while skating on irregular sidewalks as a child.

Yet I continued to clamp on my skates with my key, regardless of my clumsiness. I kept on skating because I found a sense of freedom in the sport.

For the sake of nostalgia, Sharon thought I needed another skate key. She was right.

I often think about my carefree roller-skating days in Akron, Ohio. Along the way, I discovered that country kids considered sidewalk skating a citified undertaking—and that they envied us.

We city girls wore our skate keys on ribbons around our necks. Boys wore theirs on twine or old shoelaces; but more often, they kept the keys in their pockets.

I recall skating on the slate sidewalks along Adolph and Arch streets, near Akron City Hospital. Most of those slick walkways were extremely irregular due to the large tree roots that pushed them out of position. Those walks weren't the safest course for skating. But I jumped across the obstacles in much the same way as modern skateboarders perform their antics.

I did lots of skating—on May Street in South Akron, and before that, on Kenmore Boulevard in Kenmore, Ohio. I think I fell more than I stayed upright.

But still, my skating memories are good ones. I hang the skate key from a pretty blue ribbon to remind me of my klutzy but Good Old Days. ❖

Sounds of the Neighborhood

By Caroline Ray

Recently I returned to the neighborhood where I grew up in the 1940s. With one century ended and a new millennium begun, I was curious to see if anything of my past remained. I was comforted to see that the street looked the same. The little white houses still stood all in a line like toy soldiers, with a new generation of children running from yard to yard.

I walked down the block, taking it all in, wondering who that was going into Betty Drane's house. Where were the sounds of Mr. Browning's sawing and hammering? Who were those kids in my front yard? I watched them dangling their feet and dipping their hands into my fishpond—the pond my father had dug so many years ago as I followed every step he took.

Suddenly I felt as if I were surrounded by ghosts of my past. I seemed to float through a fog back to 1942.

> *It was safe, and there was a feeling of belonging, a sense of ownership.*

Growing up on Beecher Street in the south end of Louisville, Ky., in the 1940s was fun. It was safe, and there was a feeling of belonging, a sense of ownership. It was *my* street, with *my* friends, in *my* neighborhood.

Many young couples lived there, raising their families. But there were also a few older people on our block, and they were like grandparents to all of us. They looked out for us, and we cared about them. We ran errands for them, and we raked their yards, shoveled their sidewalks and did whatever chores little people could do. In return, they always had a cookie and a smile for us. We never took money; our parents would have disapproved of that.

Summer evenings were gathering time for us under the streetlight in front of Carol and Donna's house. During the school year, the streetlight was the signal to get ourselves home. But in the summer, man, that was freedom time! We could play out until our parents called us in. We told ghost stories and played games like hide-and-seek; calls of "Five, ten, fifteen, twenty!" filled the night air. "Run, sheepie, run!" was a favorite. "Ohlie, Ohlie, home free!" was shouted over and over as we sneaked into home base.

I'll bet that on a warm June evening on Beecher Street, the sound

Facing page: *Raking Leaves With Grandpa* by John Slobodnik © House of White Birches nostalgia archives

of "Ohlie, Ohlie, home free!" can be heard by kids today. They may even feel the whisk of one of us as we slip in to home.

In 1948, my friends and I became 12 years old, and the old games seemed too childlike. We took up other things to occupy our evenings. We walked to the drugstore for a 5-cent cherry Coke, or we sat on Betty Sue's porch, talking about movie stars and boys, and watching our little brothers and sisters play the games we had abandoned.

On our walks, familiar sounds accompanied us, reassuring sounds that we had heard every summer night of our young lives. Mrs. Cunningham's squeaky swing had a soothing rhythm to it. The hammering and sawing coming from Mr. Browning's garage was as much a part of the night as the darkness itself.

Sounds from the radio were always in the background, muddled sounds of dozens of stations. During the World Series, we never had to go indoors to listen. The game could be heard all up and down the street.

On Friday nights, our father brought the radio out into the yard to listen to the Gillette Friday night fights. We would all gather on Betty Sue's porch to listen to the fights too. We absolutely loved the announcer's deep voice, and we cheered as he would get excited at a knockdown. It didn't matter who went down; we just wanted to listen to him shout.

But nothing about the fights was as much

1935 Emerson radio photo, House of White Birches nostalgia archives

fun as the commercials. We sang along at the top of our lungs: "To look sharp, use Gillette blue blades, to feel sharp, use Gillette blue blades." The fun of it was in saying "blue blades." It took a certain jaw movement and a rolling of the tongue. Danny Fowler was the best "blue blader" you ever heard.

We never outgrew this particular pastime. We gathered until television came along and drove our fathers inside. I wonder: Do the children of Beecher Street on a Friday evening sometimes hear a chorus of young people roaring out "blue blades"?

Summer evenings in bed—after a long night of games, fighting mosquitoes and a hot bath to wash off "grass itch"—were filled with comforting sounds. Mom and Dad murmuring as they prepared for bed and the sound of Mom winding the clock were such safe, homey sounds. They seemed to say "We love you. We'll be together, safe and sound, forever." The chirping crickets, I pretended, were telling me goodnight, and the owl down the street seemed to be calling to someone.

The steady rhythm of my dog, Skippy, breathing was a comfort that all too soon I was to lose. The rumble and lonesome whistle of a train made me snuggle down and dream of places I would go.

The children of Beecher Street surely must hear the same whistle and rumbling of a train. And they, too, must snuggle down to dream. ❖

Silver and Red in the Rain

By Marie Pietsch Imlay

I loved growing up on the Lower East Side of New York in the 1940s and '50s. My neighborhood was predominantly Irish and German, as am I. When I was growing up in a tenement, the sidewalks of New York were my playground. I played stickball on side streets. I played Kick the Can and King of the Hill. The boys and I pitched pennies against a wall, and whoever got closest to the wall won all the pennies. I was good at that game.

When my friends weren't available, I'd play stoopball, throwing my Spaldeen against the steps and catching it. I was a tomboy, although my mother insisted on dressing me in frilly dresses, with Shirley Temple curls and big bows in my blond hair. How I hated those bows!

Sunday in the city was my favorite day. When I opened my eyes in the morning, I would lie very still and listen. There was a hush over the city. Gone was the hustling, bustling noise of Eighth Avenue. The office buildings across the street were empty. The workers were nowhere to be found. I could hear the *tap-tap-tap* of the dog upstairs as his nails made music on the linoleum.

The best Sundays were rainy ones in the fall. My Sundays, of course, started with Mass at St. Bernard's, followed by tea and toast at the corner soda fountain. Tea and toast has never tasted quite as good since I've grown up.

In those kinder, gentler days, I had a good deal of freedom for a girl of 10. As an only child, I learned to entertain myself, and I didn't mind solitude. On Sundays, with my parents' permission, I would take a long walk alone. Mother would smile sweetly, and Dad would give me my safety warnings.

With the rain gently falling, I would don my silver raincoat with the hood and my bright red boots, stick my hands in my pockets and begin my stroll through the city. The hood kept my Shirley Temple curls dry. I felt pretty.

The rain made the city smell clean and fresh. Since the stores were always closed on Sundays, only a few people were out, walking beneath brightly colored umbrellas. But not me; I had a beautiful silver raincoat, my hood and my bright red boots—and the city was all mine.

With rain falling and wind whipping around each corner, I walked down Eighth Avenue to 13th Street, turned left at the library and made my way toward Washington Square Park. I walked through Greenwich Village, stopping to peer through the rain-covered shop windows—especially at the "gypsy" jewelry store, full of dangling earrings and shiny bracelets. *Someday I'll pierce my ears and wear beautiful long earrings,* I'd say to myself.

On Sundays, with my parents' permission, I would take a walk alone.

There were two blocks in the Village that always took my breath away. The buildings were set far back from the sidewalk, surrounded by courtyards, trees, flowers and statues. It was beautiful, and I wanted to live there. I just knew that was where the rich people lived. *Someday, I'll live there too,* I vowed to myself.

Finally I reached Washington Square, with its large, French-looking arch and the great fountain in the middle of the park. The rain fell gently. The park was empty.

The brightly colored leaves were beginning to fall—red, yellow, gold and brown—at my feet. My city, my park, my jeweled leaves, my very own day. I watched the falling rain make ripples in the fountain, then turned and started my walk back to my tenement.

The rain gently kissed my face. My cheeks tingled. I was happy. I was walking in New York City in the rain. I was free.

I had a silver raincoat and bright red boots. I was 10, and I felt pretty. ❖

Neighborhood Park

By David Anderson

When I was growing up in the 1940s, we had a wonderful little park called Pottawattomie in our neighborhood on the far north side of Chicago. My sister, our friends and I spent many beautiful summer afternoons there, absorbed in a variety of activities. The park occupied about half a city block and was bounded on three sides by tall, deep shrubs that muffled the street noise and afforded a sense of seclusion. Three paths cut through the park and were lined at intervals with benches. Between these paths were sections of grass with many big old trees. A large rectangular section along one side of the park was clear of trees and was used for playing games.

Our playground was at the back of the park, behind a long row of bushes, and beyond it lay a large expanse of victory gardens. Some of these gardens, neglected since the war ended, had grown up in weeds and beautiful wildflowers. I loved to swing as high as I could and look out over the gardens, glimpsing butterflies flitting and gliding over the flowers.

Just outside the playground was a drinking fountain. There, after drinking our fill, we watched with fascination as blue-black mud daubers gathering balls of mud at the edges of the puddles and flew off to their nests.

Our park had a quaint little field house too, where we would sometimes take our checkers or dominoes and play on the front stoop. Or a group of us would check out the croquet set, with its eight brightly colored balls and matching mallets, and set up the wickets on the open lawn. What fun it was to whack a colorful ball through a wicket or into another ball!

We also attended scheduled craft workshops in the field house, making pot holders, change purses, comb cases and other accessories. I loved making pot holders in different color combinations and designs. Putting a nickel in an old coffee can, I told Mrs. Boldenau, the park supervisor, how many jersey loops of each color I wanted. After counting them out carefully from large boxes, she handed me my loops and a small square loom and hook. Children of all ages sat around long tables, some quietly concentrating, others talking and laughing as they worked.

It was such fun to finish and admire another attractive pot holder. Two or three times during the summer, when I'd made enough pot holders for a nice selection, I took them around to neighbor ladies in my building and sold them for 5 cents apiece.

One summer, when I was older, a neighbor girl and I took marimba lessons at the field house. Learning marimba was easy for us since we both were taking piano lessons and already could read music. At the end of the summer, kids from our class joined others from other parks in a citywide marimba concert in the auditorium of one of the city's largest field houses.

Some of my fondest memories of Pottawattomie Park are of the outdoor story hours held in the summers by Miss Federgren, the children's librarian from our local library. Once a week she walked six blocks from the library to the park, accompanied by a throng of kids who'd either left with her or joined en route. My sister and I anxiously waited with a group at the park until some kid called, "Here she comes!" Then, sitting on the grass beneath the spreading limbs of the park's largest tree, we listened spellbound to her dramatic retellings of such stories as *The Elves and the Shoemaker, Rumpelstiltskin* and *The Princess and the Pea*. Even though we'd heard many of the tales before or read them ourselves, we were always glad to hear them again.

Of course, we filled our joyful summer days with other activities too. We went to the beach, took a trip to Riverview, Chicago's great amusement park, or just played games in our large, paved backyard. But for me, the most enriching and rewarding times were the afternoons we spent at our neighborhood park. ❖

Stickball

By Harry B. Peace

I am 89, and I spent my youth in New York City. From the time I was 8 until I was 18 (1926–1936), my friends and I played a game called "stickball." We played it seven days a week. We played it on school playgrounds with high fences, and we played it in the streets. We played other schools too. Sometimes we even had a school league. Schools promoted stickball because it helped keep energetic young boys out of trouble.

When we played stickball at school, on the fenced playground, we played with nine players per team, just like baseball. We used the same rules as baseball too, with some exceptions. Our bat was a broomstick that had been taped up along the hitting end. Many kids made and kept their own. The ball was a tennis ball. We fielded with our bare hands—no gloves.

As for bases, we used whatever we could find. Sometimes we marked home plate with chalk. The pitcher had to throw the ball over the plate on one bounce. No fastballs were allowed. The batter was out after one swinging strike or two foul balls. The batter was allowed to let a pitch go by, though, without penalty. No balls were called.

Runners had to stay on base till a ball was hit—there were no stolen bases. Nor could the hitter get on base by being hit by a pitch. There were no ground-rule doubles. We swung for the fences and tried to hit for everything we could get. Boys who could hit home runs out over the tall fences around the schoolyard were our heroes.

When we played on the street, the same rules applied, but we needed only six players per team: two infielders, two outfielders, a pitcher and a catcher. And if we were short of players, we played anyway. There were no umpires, volunteers or team captains.

And there were no girls. They played hopscotch. ❖

Dish Night at the Movies

By Ferne Smith Neeb

Eva was waiting for me on her front porch when I came home from school. My parents called our neighbors "Harry" and "Eva." We children called them "Mr. and Mrs. Miller." We lived side by side in one of four double houses on our block in Northampton, Pa.

"Will you go to the movies for me tonight?" Eva asked. I asked how I could go for her. "It's dish night, and my rheumatism hurts too much to walk six blocks to the Roxy," she replied.

I had never heard of "dish night." Our family rarely went to the movies. I was fortunate to get to the Shirley Temple pictures.

Eva took me into her dining room to explain dish night. She showed me a set of beautiful white china decorated with red roses and gold trim. "I got these, one piece each week, at the Roxy two years ago. This year's set is a modern style, and it's so pretty. They have one on display in the lobby."

I hurried home to ask Mother's permission to go to a movie for Eva's dish. "I'd rather you were in bed by nine on a school night," she said, "but Eva is a good neighbor. You may go just this once."

Eva gave me 30 cents, the admission price

for an adult. "I'm not 14 yet," I said. "I only need 15 cents."

"You'll have to pay adult admission to get a dish," Eva explained. "I know you'll be careful with it."

Mother suggested I take a bag to put the dish in. I was more concerned about which actress I might see—Carole Lombard, Bette Davis, Janet Gaynor, Katharine Hepburn or Ginger Rogers? My older sister had pictures of all these, and male stars, too, all over her bedroom walls.

The line at the theater was long—and mostly women. I looked for a classmate to sit with but found none.

I don't remember the name of the movie I saw, but I remember the dish. I held on to it as if it were a queen's tiara. It was yellow with a gold rim and a black silhouette on one side. It reminded me of pictures I had seen of men sitting in a booth at a British pub. Eva was right. It was attractive and different.

I felt quite grown-up when I got to bed that night. I had been an adult for two hours, and I had delivered the prized dish safely to Mrs. Miller.

"That will probably never happen again," I yawned as I fell asleep. But Eva needed help a few more times, especially on snowy nights, when it wasn't safe for her to be out. One night I saw Claudette Colbert in *Imitation of Life*. That film is still a favorite. I also liked *San Francisco*, about the 1906 earthquake and fire.

By the time I was in high school and had a little spending money from baby-sitting, World War II was in progress and dish night was no more. When Bob and I married in 1952, we bought our china at a shop in Ohio for much more than 30 cents a piece. As we paid for service for eight, I longed for the Good Old Days. ❖

Jeff Davis Hill

By Janet H. Payson

The South and its ways of life changed a great deal during the 1950s, but I was not aware of it as I was growing up on Jeff Davis Hill. I lived there until I was 18 years old. The name of my street was really Jeff Davis Avenue, but because our house sat at the top of the incline, we called it Jeff Davis Hill. The street was named, of course, for Jefferson Davis. It was one of the first avenues built and developed beyond the original downtown area of Montgomery, Ala. Huge old trees lined the street, and the sidewalks were made of concrete blocks laid in a pattern so that every other center block was blue. Some of the blocks had been pushed up and out of place by spreading tree roots. I remember these distinctly because they created quite a hazard for the neighborhood children when they skated down the walk.

Stores stood at both ends of the block. They were primarily food stores, but they were quite unlike the chain grocery stores of today. Each had been in existence for quite some time. Each had a wooden floor; an old-fashioned metal, chest-type drink box; and a long meat case across the back. The storeowners were also the butchers. When we wanted to purchase meat, we waited patiently until the owner finished his clerking duties at the front of the store.

> *On sweltering afternoons, we sat and played in the shade on the big wooden porches of our homes.*

My family's home, like most of that time, had no air-conditioning. On sweltering summer afternoons, we sat and played in the shade on the big wooden porches of our homes.

When we tired of play, we cooled off by going to one of the stores to get a cold drink from the enormous drink box. The relief of reaching into its icy depths was always sweet but brief. I always thought those drink boxes were like treasure chests where orange, grape and strawberry pop sparkled like gems amid the glittering ice.

Drinks in hand, we walked back up the hill, soothing our dry throats and planning to save the bottles until we needed to cash them in for sweet treats (like when we had run out of allowance money).

Life was never boring on Jeff Davis Hill. We played outdoors from early morning until sometimes 10 o'clock at night, stopping only for meals and chores. Each summer, we built playhouses, forts and clubhouses that stayed intact until September school days. We built them in the empty fields behind our houses or in the bamboo-cane thickets around our neighborhood.

There were plenty of children to divide into teams for softball, croquet and cards. Our homes' porches provided shady havens from the heat of summer afternoons.

Every porch had a swing to crowd onto. We spent hours there, singing rounds such as *Row, Row, Row Your Boat* in loud voices that stirred the still afternoon.

When darkness fell, winter and summer, we always played hide-and-seek. "Base" was the rickety wooden steps that led to the back of the Simmons house next door. I guess we chose that yard because it afforded more hiding places than others did.

There was a spooky basement full of roly-poly bugs and spider crickets, plus a brick storage pit that once had been used to store canned goods and other items for winter. But now it was empty, deep and dark.

A long wisteria hedge, tall enough to crawl under, ran the length of the Simmons' drive. We never got under it in the daytime, though, because it was full of bumblebees when it was blooming.

I always had mixed feelings about being "It" when we played hide-and-seek. I hated to poke into all those dark places; I was afraid that someone other than the neighborhood children might pop out at me.

On the other hand, I loved to sit quietly on those old wooden steps, counting and staring at the spreading pecan tree opposite me. I loved that old tree. It was as special to me as all my childhood friends. I spent many hours perched in it, and I enjoyed the bountiful nuts it released each autumn. Besides that, it was beautiful against the night sky when the moon gleamed through its branches. I associated it with safety and peacefulness. To this day, I am engulfed by these same feelings whenever I see a gracious, spreading old tree.

Life on Jeff Davis Hill was special, imbued with a simple splendor. None of us ever wanted for the bare necessities of food, clothing and comfortable homes.

We shared a wonderful abundance of love, and care for and from our families and one another. Little did we know that our simple happiness was the most precious and sought-after thing in life.

Nor did we ever dream that the passing years would steal it all away, separate us and end it all as they also ended our childhood. ❖

1958 *Wee Wisdom* cover from the collection of Janice Tate

The Elusive Prize

By Susan C. Barto

I knew a bubble-gum machine stood inside the entrance of the barbershop where my friends and I got our hair cut. We lived in the Ocean Parkway and Kings Highway section of Brooklyn, N.Y., circa 1947. We often dropped in to buy a piece of bubble gum.

One day, Cookie came running over to me. "The bubble-gum machine has prizes! Sometimes you get a prize along with the gum!" she said. I had never seen prizes in a bubble-gum machine before. I dashed over to the barbershop with Cookie to check it out. Sure enough, several prizes glittered among the brightly colored gum. But there were many more pieces of gum than there were prizes.

How I coveted a prize! The idea of getting something for free was irresistible. I planned to plunk every penny I received into the machine. Cookie held a penny, and then it disappeared inside the machine. Only a couple of blue gum balls dropped out of the slot.

I walked home, thinking that I'd ask my mother for a couple of pennies to try my luck. My mother gave me three and smiled tolerantly. As I headed toward the barbershop with my three pennies, I ran into my friends from the neighborhood and my cousin Andy. So far, no one had won a prize.

When I reached the bubble-gum machine, I held my breath, closed my eyes for luck, and plopped the first penny into the slot. Only gum came back out. I did the same with the next two pennies. When I had finished, I held a myriad of colorful gum balls.

The author and her friends.

Over the next week, my friends and I tried to win the elusive prizes. Then, beginning with Andy, my friends gradually began to win. Every once in a while, just often enough to keep me hoping, someone won one of the tiny gifts.

One day I changed a nickel from my allowance into pennies to put into the machine. That barbershop held me prisoner, just as a gambler is held prisoner in Las Vegas in front of the slot machines. "Once you win, you don't think the prize is important anymore," my cousin Andy said. That might be true, but I wanted to prove it myself. I kept trying to get a prize whenever I had spare pennies from my allowance. But still I failed to find a prize among the gum balls that fell from the machine's mouth.

One day, while walking home from school, I spied a penny on the ground. *Maybe this penny will bring me luck,* I thought. *Maybe this penny isn't jinxed.* I ran all the way to the barbershop, clutching my find in my fist. I pushed the penny into the slot and waited to see what would happen. When the gum dropped, a glint of metal shone between the gum balls.

At last! I discovered a tin ring with a fake blue stone shining. I was thrilled with the ring, cheap or not. It just fit my pinkie finger. The joy of winning it made me remember it always.

Years later, I noticed that some gum-ball machines contained only prizes. And the gum-ball machines that did contain gum had more prizes than gum! I thought then that no child could experience the feeling I'd had when I finally got that elusive prize! ❖

Riverside Telephone Company

By John Tissot

Stand on any street corner in any town or city in this country today for five minutes, and chances are you will see at least three people with small, funny-shaped objects held up to their ears and mouths. Americans are fascinated by the idea of communicating by means of gadgets and gizmos.

As kids, my brother and I tied a string between two tin cans, stretched the string between the back porch and the middle of the backyard and talked to each other. I imagine that other children did the same. Would children of today do this when TV and computers beckon?

The kids on my block in Riverside, Calif., had another system for talking to each other. "Our Leader," as we called him, was a man we thought of as old; looking back, he may have been in his 20s. We didn't know much about him, but we knew he was a ham-radio operator, and that meant he talked to people all over the world. He also helped us kids create our own communications system.

First, we had to get our parents to buy us each a set of earphones. Then, with the help of Our Leader, we strung a copper wire from one earphone to another. The other wire of the earphone had to be grounded, which usually meant we tied it to a water pipe or some such.

The copper wire that went from phone to phone had to be strung along back fences. Every house had a back fence then. Kids on both sides of the street were hooked up, so the wire must have crossed Elmwood Street at some point, from a tall tree on one side to a tall tree on the other, high over the street.

We kids couldn't understand how voices could go from home to home without electricity. Our Leader, who was older and a ham operator, said the earth's natural electric force would do it. If he said it would work, it would. And it did.

Most of us kids rested our earphones on tables near our beds. My room was upstairs, so both wires went across my room and out the window. One was tied to a water pipe. The other angled down to the roof of our garage.

I still remember the excitement of that day. From the roof, the wire somehow went across our backyard to the back fence and then, back fence to back fence, up the street to the next phone. There may have been 10 of us hooked up.

Our agreement was that we'd pick up the earphones at 8 o'clock.

Without electricity, there was no way of "ringing up" the other kids, but our standing agreement was that we'd pick up the earphones at about 8 o'clock in the evening, close to our bedtime. The fact that we could talk secretly to our friends while we lay in bed fascinated us.

Please recall that this occurred during the 1930s, when the world offered fewer attractions than today. On summer evenings, we would play Kick the Can, then go off to our bedrooms to talk to our friends for another 10 or 15 minutes.

We must have kept our line up for at least a year. Sometimes a line would go dead; then, the next day, we'd have to trace the wire from fence to fence to find and repair the break. Our Leader didn't have to help us much unless the break occurred out of our reach, like high in a tree.

We youngsters didn't give our communications system a name. If we'd thought of it, we probably would have called it the Riverside Telephone Company. ❖

That's Entertainment!

Chapter Two

The fact that drive-ins have been around for over 75 years pretty much has been lost upon the younger generation. The first drive-in movie in America was shown in Camden, N.J., on June 6, 1933. There were only about 150 drive-ins in this country at the end of World War II, but by 1958 there were nearly 5,000.

I remember the drive-in with great passion—not because of the "Passion Pit" label that was put on it in the 1950s, but because it was the site of some of my most memorable family outings when I was a youngster.

If you ask me, then or now, I would exclaim, "Now *that's* entertainment!"

Why did the drive-in phenomena catch on like a prairie wildfire back in the Good Old Days? I'm no sociologist, but I know all the reasons it caught on in our family.

First, it was a great way to cap off a Saturday in the city. Visits to the city were rather rare, but we tried to make those infrequent trips special. What better way to do that than seeing a movie? When we went to a movie as a family, it was always to the drive-in, mainly because my father was a smoker, and of course, smoking was not allowed in an indoor theater.

The drive-in was cheaper as well. The Camden, N.J., drive-in charged 25 cents for the car and 25 cents per person up to three people. If you had three or more in the car, they charged a flat-rate dollar. That was the birth of the carload concept. Our drive-in had a carload price, although I can't remember how much it was. I know that Daddy calculated it to be a

Years later, when I graduated to driving status, that flat rate became an invitation to see how many people you could cram into a car.

lot cheaper than two adult and three children admissions at the walk-in movie house.

Years later, when I graduated to driving status, that flat rate became an invitation to see how many people you could cram into a car. Some even tried secreting passengers in the trunk.

Do you remember the open space between the drive-in screen and the first row of cars? For a long time it was wasted turf. That was until the advent of the baby boom in the late 1940s when drive-ins began to erect playground equipment there to entice families to frequent the show.

It was a brilliant move! Our family—along with tens of thousands like us—began to show up early for the show. Many drive-ins opened three hours before showtime. We kids would go wear ourselves out on the playground while the adults talked. The concession stands began to offer chicken, barbecue and hamburgers in addition to their normal snacks.

When the show finally started, we youngsters were able to stay awake for the first feature and a cartoon or two, but were sound asleep before the double- or triple-feature evening was finished.

If I had a nickel for every time Daddy carried me into the house … . Well, I wouldn't be a rich man, but I *am* a lot richer for having had drive-ins as entertainment back in the Good Old Days.

I hope the stories in this chapter remind you of those times when urban venues of all sorts—from amusement parks and fairs to carnivals and movie houses—made us laugh, scream and cry out loud: "That's entertainment!"

—Ken Tate

Coney Island

By Joyce Normandin

When I was just a small child, before we moved from the middle Hudson Valley to Brooklyn, N.Y., my family often traveled to Bay Ridge to visit friends. Our summer visits always included a trip to Coney Island. We went to the beach or visited the amusement parks. One trip included Luna Park. I just loved it; it was a highlight of our visit. Unfortunately, Luna Park burned down and was not rebuilt.

When we finally made the move in 1942, Coney Island remained a special outing. We took the subway to Coney, and the trip seemed to take hours because we were so anxious to get there. As soon as we got off the subway, we knew that we had left the heat and humidity of the city behind as the wonderful sea breeze and salt air washed over us.

Mom always packed a lunch, an old blanket and some towels if we were spending the day at the beach. We couldn't wait to get in the water! Jumping into the waves, we squealed as the cold water splashed our sun-warmed skin.

Coney Island Beach was often very crowded. We had to go early in the morning to stake a claim to a small bit of sand. All around us, folks in colorful bathing suits were lying in the sun on their blankets. Some of them brought beach umbrellas. Kids running past kicked up the sand. Portable radios played everywhere.

Everyone seemed to have a picnic basket full of food. An ice-cream man plied the beach, selling his wares. We could go to a place under the Boardwalk to buy soda to drink with our sandwiches or ice cream. Then we'd sit on the sand, slurping away. We never went back in the water until an hour had passed. While we waited, we could watch the Parachute ride at Steeplechase Park. Many times people got stuck up on the top of the ride for what seemed like hours.

Mom and her friends—or sometimes my Aunt Marian—would settle in, reading a book while they kept an eye on us through their sunglasses. In the meantime, we splashed in the water or built sand castles with our little pails and shovels.

Once we decided to sit under the Boardwalk, out of the sun. But the sand from hundreds of feet passing overhead filtered down onto us, and we had to retreat out onto the beach again.

Coney Island in the Good Old Days.

Returning home, I drifted off to sleep on the old caned seats of the swaying, rumbling subway, exhausted from my day in the sun, sand and seawater.

It was a special treat when Dad and Mom announced that we were going to Coney Island for the rides and fun. We arrived there in the afternoon and stayed until after night fell.

Getting off the subway, we headed for Surf Avenue, glowing with colored lights and thick with crowds. Here there were all kinds of games and sideshows. You could try to knock down wooden bottles with a baseball, pitch balls into metal rings on a board, or toss rope rings onto bottles for prizes. I never could do it, but Dad occasionally won a prize. Then I would go home hugging a stuffed animal or doll.

There were barkers who claimed they could guess your weight or age. Some men tried to hit a board with a sledgehammer hard enough to drive a mechanism up to ring a bell. And penny arcades abounded; there, for just a penny, you could watch old silent-movie shorts.

All along the avenue there were "freak shows" and sideshows featuring unusual attractions like the fat lady, the bearded lady, the rubber man and the sword swallower. The sideshow barkers stood out front, dressed in straw hats and striped shirts, urging one and all to go in. But we never did—and I am sure I missed something really wonderful. (I was rather ghoulish at that age.)

We always stopped at my favorite merry-go-round. While Mom and Dad settled on a bench, I whirled around and around. I enjoyed at least three rides while trying to catch the brass ring, which meant a free ride.

Then we would walk over to Nathan's Hot Dogs. Everyone knew that they were the best on Coney Island. Mom and I sat at a small table inside while Dad bought our hot dogs, smeared with mustard, and cold root beer, all foamy on top and served in huge glass mugs that looked like steins.

After finishing our food, we would walk along the street to take in more amusements and sights. One place had small ponies that you could ride around in a small ring. How I loved that pony ride! I never got enough of it. Having seen all those old Western movies, I could pretend that I was a cowgirl riding the range. The pony moved at a snail's pace, but that never stopped my imagination from working overtime.

Next was the Cyclone, Dad's favorite ride. Mother never went; she said she didn't like it. But I think that that was just an excuse so I could go with Dad. Dad and I took lots of rides together. We rode the cars in the Whip, which spun us around and around. I sat next to Dad in the electric bumper cars. We would bump into other riders, and they in turn would steer to bump into us.

The Cake Walk was a popular attraction at Luna Park. Luna Park burned when the author was a child and was not rebuilt.

We also rode the Thunderbolt, a type of roller coaster. You just could not go to Coney Island and not ride a roller coaster! We held our stomachs, screaming as we hurtled to the bottom, only to climb another peak and plunge down again, hair flying in the breeze.

Next, we would go to the Boardwalk where there were food stands like the ones on Surf Avenue. Hot corn on the cob was always tasty, as were the greasy French fries served in a paper cup. We would stroll along as we munched, or find a beach looking out over the ocean and eat.

Frozen custard was a treat. Nowadays, soft ice cream is easily available, but back then, a big cone filled with frozen custard was special indeed. It was rich and creamy, and I have never since had any that was so delicious. My favorite flavor was banana. We never went to Coney Island without me getting a chance to enjoy it.

Of course, we also had to have some pink cotton candy and get our faces and hands all sticky. We knew it would be hot and humid when we got home, but standing at the rail on the Boardwalk, looking out to the ocean, we felt cool in the breeze.

Some folks rode along the Boardwalk in big, rented wheeled chairs with caned seats, large enough to hold two or three people. They looked like huge baby carriages with a handle on the back. You rode along the Boardwalk in comfort, pushed from behind by the operator who rented the contraption. Lots of elderly folks took advantage of this, but many younger ones did too.

My uncle told us that when he shipped out for England, his ship was torpedoed not far from Long Island and had to return to the dock for repairs. It's a good thing we didn't know about it at the time; we all would have been scared. We didn't learn about it until after the war. But we could watch the ships plying their way out of the harbor, bound for faraway places. There were rumors that Nazi submarines were in New York Harbor, but we never did find out if they were true.

Sometimes we took a trip to Coney Island just to visit Steeplechase Park, owned by the Tilyou family. A ticket for six rides cost 50 cents, and a $1 ticket gave you 12 rides. These round tickets had spots to be punched as you took each ride.

We could spend a day at Steeplechase Park and never lack for things to do or see. At the entrance was a huge wooden barrel, open at both ends, which rotated constantly. The trick was to walk through the barrel without falling. It didn't take long to learn that it was best to go through as quickly as possible. Steeplechase had outdoor rides and many more inside a huge building; that was great because when it rained, we could continue our fun inside.

One feature inside was a very wide wooden slide that reached all the way to the ceiling. Once we'd reached the bottom, clowns with what looked like low-voltage cattle prods herded us to the exit. Breezes rose from the floor in puffs to blow up the ladies' skirts. In front of the exit were rows of seats where folks could rest and watch the fun and laugh at the clowns.

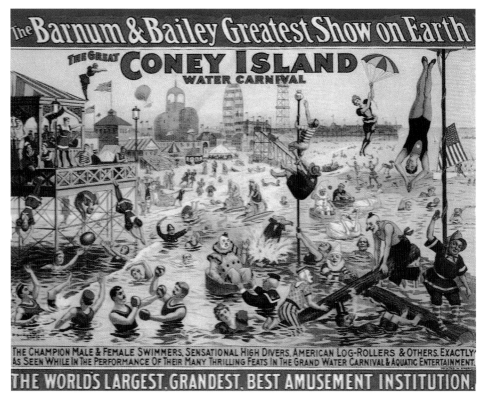

Barnum & Bailey's Great Coney Island Water Carnival was a seasonal attraction. It brought champion swimmers, sensational high divers and other thrilling feats.

Another fun ride was a huge wooden bowl with a hump in the center. Riders started out sitting on the hump, then the bowl rotated faster and faster. The trick was to stay in the middle as long as possible, but as the bowl spun, centrifugal force eventually sent everyone to the bottom.

Outside, around the edge of the building's roof, were mechanical horses. We pretended our horses were racing as we rode the circuit around. A large Ferris wheel gave us a wonderful view of Steeplechase, the Boardwalk, the beach, the ocean and Surf Avenue. We would go back to the barrel at the entrance several times and practice walking through without falling down.

I wanted to try the Parachute, but I never had the courage. Riders ascended to the top where cables were released, the parachutes opened, and they floated gently down—theoretically, anyway. Aunt Marian, who sometimes had more courage than common sense, climbed up one time, but her parachute got stuck, and we spent some time peering up at her as she dangled there. Always a glutton for punishment, she went up again later that same afternoon—and she convinced Dad to go with her. Fortunately, the chutes worked properly this time.

Steeplechase had a merry-go-round and a Whip ride, as well as those electric bumper cars. In fact, just about every type of outdoor ride could be found indoors at Steeplechase. Lots of food concessions gave us a choice of treats too.

It seems that we never went to Coney Island alone. Friends or family always went with us, and it was great to share the fun, food and thrills.

Unfortunately, the Coney Island we knew back then no longer exists. Luna Park is gone, and I have been told that Steeplechase closed down years ago too. Someone told me that there is an aquarium at Coney Island now. That may be interesting, but I'll bet it's not as much fun as a roller coaster.

Coney Island was where I first got a chance to watch television, as it was playing inside a restaurant. It's where pony rides let me live my cowgirl dreams. It was where I ate the best frozen custard on the planet, and where I finally caught my very first brass ring on the merry-go-round. Perhaps it was gaudy, crowded, noisy and garish. Maybe we often came home from the beach sunburned, with sand in our shoes. But we loved every inch of it. ❖

Times Square

By Rowena Stuart

What's the difference between the ages of 5 and 15? Well, for one thing, tastes change. So it was with my sister and me. When we were growing up in the early 1940s, Sunday afternoons usually meant a short subway ride to Times Square with our father. It meant going to the penny arcade, the Laff Movie, the Horn & Hardart Automat, and then the ride home. We looked forward to it—when we were 5 and 6, or even at 10 and 12. After that, it became passé to go to those places with Daddy.

I don't know exactly the year that we stopped looking forward to it. I don't know exactly when we went for our own enjoyment, or when we went to please our father. He never stopped enjoying it. So we kept going.

The Horn & Hardart Automat. Inset: Penny arcade cards of Louis Hayward, Franchot Tone and Mamie Van Doren.

The change was slow and subtle; one day my mother said to him, "Maybe skip this week and let the girls be with their friends." I know Daddy did his best to hide his disappointment.

When Daddy was young and movies were new, the Charlie Chaplin pictures were a scream. Films also featured Buster Keaton, the Three Stooges and other early entertainers. In the darkened theater, we would steal a glance or two at Daddy laughing at the slapstick flickers. Those movies brought back his childhood, his youth, and he laughed with abandon.

And the penny arcade was fun—for a while. We loved the giant, fake fortune-teller; for a coin, it would drop a card with your future on it.

The Horn & Hardart Automat was nice—we were starved by the end of the day, and we really enjoyed the food there. We changed a dollar for nickels to put into the slots where beef pot pie popped out, or the baked beans—our choice.

The subway ride to Times Square and home was fast, but it didn't seem so at the time. We were tired by the end of the day.

I don't know exactly when it all ended. Sunday afternoons changed. My friends and I began to notice boys. My mother permitted me to wear Tangee lipstick—"lightly, and only on weekends, not to school."

I overheard my parents talking one day, lamenting how Times Square was "changing, going to the dogs, becoming dangerous, even during the day." I really think my father felt that was the reason we no longer went there. "Well, times change," they agreed.

Perhaps those times coincided with our age. Times Square did indeed change. But years later, it changed back to being safe and exciting. But by then, just about everything we remembered was gone. The Laff Movie, penny arcades, even the automat had all become memories.

I can still visualize it the way it used to be. What I wouldn't give for just one more visit to Times Square with my father and sister! ❖

America's Cherished Palace

By Roy Meador

Generally, the happy sound of applause comes to a stop when the audience goes home. Yet one famous American theater is a remarkable exception. The applause continues through films, fantasies, memories, legends and countless stories from the great days of vaudeville. Yes, if we listen carefully, we can still hear generations of accumulated applause for those fabulous performers who reached the summit of success when talent took them to that special theater at 47th Street and Seventh Avenue, across from Broadway in New York City.

In fact we hear 80 years of applause. March 24, 1993, was the 80th anniversary of the theater that appropriately was called the Palace, because on its stage, America's entertainment royalty proudly appeared. Soon after the Palace opened, star vaudevillians began measuring their progress and popularity by the number of times they "played the Palace." Reaching the Palace meant reaching the top.

> *"A Palace program with an act's name on it was a diploma of merit."*
> —*Fred Allen*

It was the Monday after Easter when the totally new Palace Theater offered its first eight acts of quality vaudeville at a matinee.

For that first Monday matinee, the cheapest seats cost 25 cents and the most expensive $1.50. Those were considered pretty steep prices then. But in return, the lucky audience received the standard vaudeville fare of dance, song, acrobatics and comedy.

When the Palace opened, vaudeville was the leading family entertainment medium at a time when radio and television were science-fiction dreams. Movies, though popular, were still as silent as the proverbial mouse. Thousands of vaudeville performers tirelessly toured America, mostly by train, and brought live entertainment to eager fans across the country.

Many immortals of show business were among those wandering players of long ago—Jack Benny, Eddie Cantor, Fred Allen, W.C. Fields, Fanny Brice, Sophie Tucker, Burns and Allen, Smith and Dale, Edgar Bergen, Jimmy Durante, Rudy Vallee and the Marx Brothers. The list goes on and on, a cavalcade of stars and memories. During the great years of vaudeville, all the stars played the Palace except two: Al Jolson and George M. Cohan. But even Al Jolson did sing a song once at the Palace—as a member of the audience.

Top: The Marx Brothers were regulars at the Palace. Above: The ever-funny, Ed Wynn. All photos courtesy House of White Birches nostalgia archives.

And long after the passing of vaudeville, when the Palace had become what it is today, a handsome theater for Broadway musicals, the musical about the life of George M. Cohan, *George M!*, was staged at the Palace. So eventually, even Cohan played the Palace.

The Palace during its first week offered nine acts. Eight or nine acts was the customary bill in a vaudeville house. As part of the big-time vaudeville circuit, the Palace offered two shows daily—the famous two-a-day.

On the small-time circuit, which included thousands of humbler theaters nationwide, five or six shows per day was the usual billing. Small-time performers were like ballplayers in the minor leagues. They gained experience and honed their skills so they would be ready when the big break came—the chance to go big time and ultimately reach the very pinnacle, the celebrated Palace.

That first week set a pattern the Palace used with great success for decades, until talking boxes in the living rooms of America and talking pictures sadly brought vaudeville to a halt.

But back then, no one was thinking about the eventual decline of vaudeville. That seemed laughably unlikely at the time.

Those who first performed at the Palace couldn't know it then. Perhaps later, some of them realized they had joined together in making history. They launched a theater that would soon be the anxious goal of every vaudeville performer in the world.

They made history and so earned the right to be remembered. Those first performers were the eight London Palace Girls, a dance act; McIntyre and Harty, a comedy team; and Hy Mayer, a *New York Times* cartoonist. There were The Four Vannis, acrobats; La Napierkowska, a dancer and pantomimist; and Ota Gygi, a violinist. A large group of performers gave a brief version of an operetta, *The Eternal Waltz*. There was a one-act play, *Speaking to Father*. There was also a skit, *The King's Jester*, in which a young vaudevillian named Ed Wynn supplied comedy.

Even if the others who first played the Palace are unknown to us today, we still remember Ed Wynn, who became a star on every entertainment medium from vaudeville to early radio, then television and movies, and still ranks

Comedian W.C. Fields once appeared at the Palace.

among the all-time great clowns. It was Ed Wynn, more than any other, who showed how to make the great leap from vaudeville to radio.

But no broadcasting studio was ever remotely the equivalent of the fabulous Palace during the glorious days of vaudeville. Groucho Marx, a vaudeville veteran from boyhood with his brothers, wrote: "The Palace Theater was the ultimate. It was the Big Time, and yet the audience was the most common. They would throw programs at the inferior

acts. (Who could afford to throw tomatoes?)" Groucho, as always, was probably exaggerating slightly for the sake of laughs. Audiences at the Palace and elsewhere were generally polite, happy and ecstatic when a great performer gave his all.

Edgar Bergen played the Palace with a wooden friend in 1929. "Vaudeville was something I liked because the audiences were so nice," he said. "We had theaters with 2,300 seats and no microphones. But people listened better and were attentive—the audience loved you even if you weren't a big star."

During that first golden spring at the Palace, Ethel Barrymore, the reigning luminary of the legitimate stage, performed in the one-act play *Miss Civilization* on the Palace bill of April 28.

Soon thereafter, the most acclaimed actress in the world, Sarah Bernhardt, climaxed a triumphant American tour by playing the Palace. Her fame and histrionics did a lot to publicize the new theater and establish it as a theater where stage monarchs liked to hold court. Madame Sarah asked for and got $1,000 cash at the time of each performance.

On the same bill with her was a juggler who later growled and gruffed his way to lasting fame as W.C. Fields.

The following year, 1914, brought Will Rogers, the Castles, Nora Bayes, Fanny Brice, Eddie Foy, Clifton Webb, Pat Rooney, Sophie Tucker and Harry Houdini, among many others, for the first time to the Palace.

In 1915, the Marx Brothers made it to the big time and the Palace. In 1916, they were on the same bill with the returning Bernhardt. She was 72 and had lost a leg, but she hadn't lost an ounce of her fighting spirit and magnificent talent. Even the zany Marx Brothers behaved themselves and showed humility in her presence.

From 1916 through the 1920s, the Palace was vaudeville's royal house. Star after star proudly appeared on stage, and each new star expanded the fame and legend of the theater.

"The Palace was the goal of every act in America," wrote Fred Allen, who played there many times. "An act that had played the Palace was booked by any theater manager in the country, sight unseen. A Palace program with an act's name on it was a diploma of merit."

Mickey Rooney and Judy Garland, 1951. Miss Garland headlined the Palace.

In the 1920s came drastic changes in the way Americans were entertained. Radio broadcasts became commonplace, and radios proliferated in homes across the nation. Many people who might have gone out to a vaudeville show began staying home and listening to the radio.

Finally, on Oct. 6, 1927, came what eventually proved to be the kiss of death for vaudeville. A moving picture called *The Jazz Singer* premiered. This wasn't just another movie; it made noises. In the film, Al Jolson talked and sang. Talking pictures won over the vast national audience that previously turned to vaudeville theaters for amusement.

Much sooner than most would have thought possible, vaudeville was largely gone by the early 1930s. Audiences and performers might have regretted its passing, but they couldn't apply the brakes to changing times.

In 1932, the Palace's two-a-day tradition was no more. The distinguished old theater began screening pictures; the day was not a happy one for vaudeville lovers.

George Jessel later spoke for vaudevillians about what was lost when vaudeville disappeared: "Vaudeville gave us great camaraderie. There were circuits where you played 20, 30 weeks with the same bill, and you became like one big family. It was warm and comfortable. You lived by the reaction of the audience. There was something warm and sweet about it."

In vaudeville theaters, audiences shared an intimate connection with performers. Audiences were important too. That's what we in the audience lost when we lost vaudeville—the feeling of importance. But all was not lost, at least not altogether. Living stars would again have their day at the Palace.

In the 1950s, the Palace reunited live audiences with live performers. On Oct. 16, 1951, Judy Garland, gloriously alive, played the Palace. Her triumph was no less than that of Sarah Bernhardt's many years earlier.

Betty Hutton, Danny Kaye, Liberace, Jerry Lewis and Harry Belafonte followed Judy Garland's lead with Palace successes during that brief resurrection.

On Nov. 26, 1956, Judy Garland returned one more time to the Palace. Police barricades were necessary to maintain control in the midst of so much love and enthusiasm. I was in the balcony as part of that grateful audience during Judy's Palace appearance.

That is a great theatrical memory time cannot dim. ❖

The Summer Carnival

By Audrey Carli

I am spinning back in time to a childhood summer in the 1940s in Wakefield, Mich. And the carnival is coming to town! I save coins from my grandparents and other relatives. Mom and Dad promise to take my two sisters, Marjorie and Myrna, my brother, Richard, and me to the grassy spot at the end of Main Street where the carnival rides will be.

The Sunday afternoon arrives. My family and I hike the five blocks to the carnival, where the fragrance of freshly mown grass touches our nostrils.

Striding along the pathways that lead to the Tilt-A-Whirl, swings, Ferris wheel and other rides, we reach the merry-go-round. We listen to the pipe-organ music that sends forth *Over the Waves* while Dad buys our tickets.

The merry-go-round moves in circles with the colorful, majestic, smooth-backed horses. Soon the ride stops and we get on. Some children smile with joy or frown with fear. Serene-faced mothers hold babies as they sit on a bench between horses.

It is joy, riding a horse to the pulsing beat of the peppy pipe organ music.

Next, we hurry to the Ferris wheel. Worry and anticipation churn in me as I await my turn on one of the wobbly seats. My sister Marjorie rides with me—and we both clutch the safety bar, hardly moving. We don't want the wobbly seat to tip over!

We catch our breath and whisper "Sit still!"

> *It is joy, riding a horse*
> *to the pulsing beat*
> *of the peppy pipe organ music.*

while we wait at the top for riders getting on and off at the bottom of the wheel. Then we are filled with adventure, joy and fear as the Ferris wheel carries us around several more times.

Our next stop is the Tilt-A-Whirl. We kids sit in the half-moon–shaped seats and clutch the locked safety bar. We are breathless as we whirl too fast. We gasp, and I worry that we might not stop spinning! But the ride slows. We are glad to get off and wonder why we got on it.

We walk along the pathways, past the games with prizes. We want to toss balls at fake milk bottles to win a fuzzy stuffed animal or even a smaller prize, but we move on instead.

The smells of popcorn and hot dogs with onions and mustard permeate the atmosphere. We walk past other displays from which shouts sound: "Cotton candy!" "Candy apples!"

As we draw near the pony rides, excitement leaps in my heart. "Please, a pony ride, Dad?"

My siblings have no interest, but Dad buys a ticket and lifts me onto the saddle. The pony plods around the circle several times as I savor my time as an Old West girl riding my horse!

Too soon, it is time to walk home again.

Our family visits the carnival once more before it disbands and moves on to the next locale on its tour.

For the rest of the summer, the grassy field reminds me of the carnival. I sense the pipe-organ music, the shouts about games, the popcorn and candy apples—and I long for next year's carnival fun! ❖

Dreamland Swimming Pool

By Gloria Dewhurst

After 50-some years, my sister Peach's friend Patty from Cincinnati came for a sentimental visit to Portsmouth. In the 1940s and 1950s, Patty's parents brought her to stay with her grandparents during the summer months when school was out. We learned to love Patty like one of the family, so we looked forward to her annual visits.

During her recent visit, Patty happened to mention how much she had enjoyed swimming at Dreamland Swimming Pool before it closed many years ago.

"I can still smell the wonderfully clean smells of chlorine and suntan lotion," she enthused.

When Peach told me about Patty's visit and her fond remembrances of Portsmouth's huge public pool, I began reminiscing about it myself.

The author, 14, at Dreamland Pool, 1948.

I remembered how excited the young children were when the pool opened each season. We would beg our parents to let us go swimming the very first day so we could brag to our friends who didn't get to go about how wonderful it was to get sunburned from staying there all day! Matter of fact, we would be so blistered that it would be a good while before they allowed us to get sunburned again.

But that pool was famous for other things besides swimming. Their hamburgers, fried fresh in the little kitchen beside the pool house, were 15 cents each. There were no fries, but a Coke cost only a nickel, so we drank one of those with our tasty burgers. Everybody loved them.

Sometimes Mr. Schirrman, who owned a music shop, played the grand piano on the second floor of the pool house. When the music drifted across the water, we felt like swimming in time with it.

When Mr. Schirrman wasn't there, a nickel in the slot of a jukebox provided music to dance by. Table tennis was also offered on the second floor for those who wanted a change of pace.

There were dressing rooms beside the entrance door, to the right for females and to the left for males. Once inside the dressing room area, we asked for wire baskets to put our clothes in. We received a safety pin with our basket number on it to pin to our swimsuits.

Then we found unoccupied dressing rooms with duck-cloth privacy curtains and changed into our suits. After we'd given the baskets containing our clothes to the attendant, we headed for the door to the pool area. Immediately outside the door was a large, shallow footbath. At another attendant's instruction, we walked through it. It contained disinfectant to ward off athlete's foot.

Now we were ready to find a spot on the lawn to put our towels or blankets. Then we dove right in and took a refreshing dip. When it was time to go home, we simply reversed the procedure. There were private showers to bathe in after our swim and built-in hair dryers.

It just so happened that Select Dairy was right around the corner from the pool. If we happened to have 5 cents left, we could buy an ice-cream cone or a double, flat-sided Popsicle. Peach and I usually opted for a double grape Popsicle to share. It tasted so good after a swim!

If you were really rich and had 20 cents in your pocket, you could stop at the Blue Pig Inn and get a frosty mug of root beer and a hot dog.

After we had climbed the hill to our home, we ate everything in the refrigerator and then lay down for a big nap, completely worn out.

I'll never forget the time Veda Mae and I went to the Midnight Swim. I begged my dad to let me go. He finally relented and said I could go if I got home by 11 p.m.

Veda Mae and I were so excited to be going to our first grown-up swim, when music played constantly on the jukebox and the lights under the pool's waters shone a beautiful blue color. It was all so glamorous!

I asked my sister-in-law, who owned a beauty shop, to style my hair in a lavish upsweep so that I would look as sophisticated as any 14-year-old girl could. Wave-set and at least a hundred bobby pins to hold it all in place did the trick. I put on my best dress and met Veda Mae. Then off we went to the Midnight Swim.

Once we were on the pool grounds, we paraded around the walkway a few times. Then I was suddenly seized with an irresistible urge to go swimming, fancy hairdo and all. Veda Mae said she didn't mind wrecking her hairdo, either, so we went swimming in that beautiful blue water. As you might have guessed, time got away from us with all the fun we were having. Now it was nearly midnight, and I'd promised Dad that I would be home by 11!

I jumped back into my street clothes in the dressing room and ran most of the way up the hill to my house. Once there, I decided to climb in the bathroom window so that my dad wouldn't know I had gotten in later than he told me to.

When the music drifted out across the water, we felt like swimming in time with it.

Well, I put one leg through the window and stepped right in the toilet and got my shoe stuck in the bowl. I was trying to retrieve my foot when the noise I was making woke Dad. He came downstairs, and of course, kind of had a fit. "Young lady," he said, "that is the last Midnight Swim you are going to! Do you realize how late it is?"

"I'm sorry," I replied. "I lost track of time after I decided to get in the water. The time just went by so fast!"

"By the way," Dad said, "I don't know why you wanted to climb in the bathroom window. The front door was unlocked."

That was the first and last Midnight Swim I ever attended. But I'm glad I had that experience, as it was lovely to swim in the pool when the underwater lights were on. I have never forgotten how beautiful it was!

Nor will I ever forget the Big Bands that played for dances at Dreamland Pool. When we found out they were playing there, all we had to do was walk one short block from home. Looking through the 6-foot chain-link fence that surrounded the pool grounds, we watched and listened to the beautiful music of Jan Garber and other famous bands.

Of course, we longed to be down there with the dancers on the grassy dance floor. But even so, just hearing this wonderful music for free was thrilling in the Good Old Days. ❖

Prospect Park

By Joyce Normandin

Prospect Park was an emerald jewel encased by the cement buildings and tarred streets that surrounded it. For the children of Brooklyn, it was a haven from the busy city streets. It was used in all seasons, from dawn till dusk—and often later by young couples who walked hand in hand along the intertwining paths in the twilight.

When I was a child in the early 1940s, my friends and I often went to the park to play. We would push our doll carriages up to the park, then stroll along Prospect Park West, feeling very important. We passed young mothers sitting on benches, gossiping, showing off their babies napping in strollers, or popping a bottle into a crying infant's mouth.

Sometimes we walked to the huge Brooklyn Public Library at Grand Army Plaza next to the park and took out books from the children's section. Then we would find a quiet nook under a tree and read. In this huge expanse of grass, we could see sunbathers listening to their portable radios and families spreading blankets for a picnic.

No matter what the season, it seemed the Brooklyn Zoo was open.

In summer, the park's wading pools were open and sprayed water on delighted children. We put on our shirts and shorts over our bathing suits and grabbed a towel, anticipating a whole afternoon there. Our moms would make sandwiches for us, and we always had some fruit or cookies to munch on. There were numerous water fountains, so we didn't have to buy drinks. At different locations there were playgrounds with swings, slides, seesaws and monkey bars.

When it was very hot, my mom often gave me some change to ride the trolley car. I think the fare was a nickel then. One of these dark red trolleys traveled up Union Street to the park. They clanged as they rode along, sparks flying from the spot where the rod connected with the cable overhead. Some boys were always climbing on the back to "hitch" a free ride.

In warm weather, the wooden sides of the trolley were taken down, and the breeze blew through, cooling all the riders as the trolley rolled along. Sometimes a bunch of us would go to the park for a game of catch or tag or hide-and-seek, or we'd just do somersaults across the grass. There was a lake there too, with pedal boats that could be rented.

In one area, a pretty stream ran downhill to another pond where we could catch pollywogs. Sometimes we would just sit on a rock and dangle our feet in the water as we wiled away a hot afternoon. On Friday nights there were free dances for teenagers at the park's Ninth Street bandstand.

In the autumn, the park's trees changed color as the days shortened and the temperatures cooled. But neither changing weather nor school prevented us from continuing our games at the park and pushing our doll carriages or riding bikes there after school. We pedaled along the park's many pathways, our bicycle baskets filled with ever-present pink Spalding balls and an apple or two.

Sometimes on Sunday afternoons we would saunter along the paths with our parents, all

The author and her mother visit Prospect Park Zoo, 1942.

dressed in our finery, as the leaves fell from the trees in an abundance of red, orange and yellow. When we went without our parents, in our "play clothes," we would build piles of leaves to jump into with abandon, smelling the autumn with each breath. Then we'd run to the water fountains for a cool drink.

Winter did indeed make a wonderland of Prospect Park. As snow covered the many hills, clutches of children hauling sleds appeared. Their shrieks resounded from the slopes as their sleds flew down the hillsides. We built snow forts, made snow angels and staged snowball fights.

We were packed into snowsuits, with scarves around our necks and woolen hats covering our ears and heads. We wore two pairs of mittens, and on our feet we pulled our dads' old socks over our shoes before we stuffed them into galoshes. Alas, we still came home with feet and hands frozen from the snow that managed to sneak inside.

As winter ebbed and the sun returned, the park warmed again, and we could see the trees budding out a bright green. Shrubs and bushes began to wake, and flowers popped up.

On Easter Sunday, it seemed that everyone we knew took advantage of the warm sunshine, walking in small groups, mothers pushing strollers, dads grasping a child by the hand. The women especially watched the "parade," eyeing the latest fashions and commenting on the Easter bonnets.

These strolls often ended in the Brooklyn Botanic Gardens, where the cherry blossoms blushed with color. One end of the park was near Ebbets Field, and we could hear the fans' shouts when a player blasted a base hit or a homer.

No matter what the season, it seemed the Brooklyn Zoo was open. It was one of my favorite trips. Nestled at one end of the park were all the lions, tigers and bears a child could wish for. My favorites were the seals and the monkeys. I could spend hours watching the yelping seals' antics as they dove into the water.

Once I said that I wished I could live in a cage with some of the animals to take care of them and be their friend. But when my uncle, who was with us at the time, picked me up and put me in an empty wire trash barrel, I quickly changed my mind.

Prospect Park may have been a great place for adults, but it was truly a paradise for children. It was a bit of the quiet countryside in the midst of a city of cement, apartment buildings and noisy streets. We never had to worry about crowded sidewalks, dodging cars or finding a place to play in the park. There it was—and it was free! Spreading its tree-lined expanses in a welcoming gesture, it offered fun for every child in every season. And it made the years 1942–1945 an unforgettable memory for me. ❖

Radio City Music Hall

By Eileen Higgins Driscoll

Radio City Music Hall is a part of Rockefeller Center—and a child of the Depression. It was built in the early 1930s as part of the Rockefeller Center Complex. And oh, what a wonderful, glamorous job they did! Since I was born in 1926, I grew up with the wonderful buildings that were built in New York City during the 1930s. The Empire State Building and the Chrysler Building were also products of that era. I was fortunate enough to work briefly in two of those buildings, and my last job in New York City was in the McGraw-Hill Building, also a part of the Rockefeller Center Complex.

My first exposure to Radio City Music Hall was with my Aunt Peggy. Everyone should have an Aunt Peggy. Aunt Peggy worked for Sinclair Oil, and their office was in the Rockefeller Center. In my world, that made her very important. She was magical!

The usher smiled at me and said, "You look just like Deanna Durbin, young lady."

When I was about 10 years old, she took me to Radio City Music Hall. I had no idea where she was taking me, but Mother did. She curled my hair as best she could, and she had my Sunday dress, coat and shoes washed, ironed, polished and ready to go. It was exciting just getting ready for our day's outing!

Aunt Peggy and I took the bus and the BMT subway from Brooklyn to Manhattan. Even the subway ride was exciting for me at that age.

When we arrived at Radio City Music Hall, there was already a long line of people waiting to buy tickets. We queued up with the rest while the handsome, uniformed ushers assured us that there were plenty of seats left. I'm going way back now, but I think they wore blue-gray uniforms with red on the collar or cape. I believe there was a touch of red on the peaked caps they wore too. At any rate, they were quite impressive to a 10-year-old girl from Brooklyn.

We finally reached the lobby. Wow! The whole lobby was white marble. A curved staircase with red padding on each step ascended to the mezzanine level. It was so big that I could hardly believe my eyes! Red velvet drapes hung over the windows. Glass chandeliers, more spectacular than any I had ever seen before, were suspended in the lobby that seemed three stories high. The gold-painted ceiling reflected the lights. It was so exciting that I wanted to dance.

We were given a program and ushered to our seats. I can't remember the name of the movie, but Deanna Durbin and Jane Withers were the stars. When the usher seated us, he smiled at me and said, "You look just like Deanna Durbin, young lady." I felt like a princess.

It was all I could do to keep from jumping up and down and yelling "Whoopee!" at the top of my lungs. I thought I'd just die of embarrassment and joy at the same time when I blushed and smiled back at him. I wonder now if he knew how happy he made a dumb kid from Brooklyn feel. He was probably all of 16 or 18 years old himself.

In a few minutes the lights went down. Then, out of the darkness, up in the air to the left of the stage, a bright light began to shine, and an organ materialized before our very eyes. A man dressed in a tux was seated at the organ, playing *Fiddle, Faddle*. I cannot hear that song today without going all the way back to that glorious day. It all seemed like magic. He played three or four numbers and ended with a John Philip Sousa march. Then the lights went out again, and the movie started.

Our plush velvet seats were big and comfortable, and we enjoyed the movie. After it was over, the magic started again. The curtain went up—and there were the Rockettes onstage! I think there were 26 girls dancing in front of us, each balanced on a big ball! They wore beautiful green costumes with matching headpieces. The girls and the balls seemed to glide around the stage with ease. How could they do that?

I could feel myself sway with the music while they performed. I remember Aunt Peggy telling me to try to stay in my seat. Nothing had ever matched the awe I felt as I watched those girls that day. I don't think I ever knew there were such beautiful things in the world.

I think Aunt Peggy enjoyed the day. I know I did. In more recent years, I have tried to be an Aunt

Peggy to other children. I hope I have succeeded half as much as my Aunt Peggy did. Every kid deserves an Aunt Peggy. ❖

Above: A view of downtown New York City, looking toward Rockefeller Center, home of Radio City Music Hall. Below: An interior view of Radio City Music Hall.

Hurry! Hurry! Hurry!

By Doris M. Kneppel

The roar of the subway, the screech of the wheels, and the smell of hot oil all helped magnify my excitement. It was really happening! Mama and I were on our way to Coney Island! It was 1932, and even more important, it was my 8th birthday. A first trip to Coney Island was the best birthday present any girl could have. I couldn't wait to see all the things my friends had described.

Mama sat opposite me, prim and beautiful, clutching her purse and the bag of lunch. I stole glances at this pretty "stranger." Mama's short, black hair dipped in soft waves around her pretty face. She had a Clara Bow mouth—pouty, soft and naturally dark pink. Her dark brown eyes sparkled with excitement when she was happy. When she smiled, it was like the sun coming out. It made me happy just to look at her! She looked so pretty in the pale blue dress she had made on her old treadle sewing machine. The light perfume she wore wafted toward me when she leaned over to speak to me.

"When the train comes into the daylight, it means we're close."

I thought I looked nice too. My best dress was also blue and looked almost new. My Sunday shoes were getting so small that my toes hurt, but they were shiny and new looking, so it didn't matter. I had combed my straight blond hair carefully, sweeping my bangs so that they hung like a fringed curtain, just brushing my eyebrows. Looking at my reflection in the train window, I decided I would never be as pretty as Shirley Temple, but I didn't mind—not today, anyway.

Reading my thoughts, Mama said, "You look really nice, Honey." She smiled and added, "We're gonna have a nice day today. We'll walk on the Boardwalk and see all the exciting things. Later we'll find a bench and eat the bologna sandwiches we brought. If I have enough money, we'll buy an orange drink. I hear they're only 3 cents. Maybe I'll even let you ride the merry-go-round, if it doesn't cost too much."

Suddenly the train burst out of the darkness and into the bright sunshine. The passengers whooped and laughed.

I must have looked confused because Mama laughed and said, "When the train comes into the daylight, it means we're close. Everybody is happy because we're almost there."

We rode high above the street. I had never been on an elevated train, and I drank in the sights and sounds, committing them to memory so that I would be able to describe them in minute detail to my friends.

The houses along the "el" train tracks seemed to lean toward us. I caught glimpses of women leaning out the windows, their arms resting on bed pillows. In one window, a little boy waved at the train. I waved back, glancing at Mama to see if she was shaking her head. (Mama always insisted on perfect behavior in public: no smiling at strangers, keeping my voice soft, and sitting like a lady—knees together, ankles crossed.) But Mama was smiling and nodding.

At every station, I looked at her expectantly, but Mama only smiled and shook her head.

Finally she grasped my hand and guided me toward the gates of the train. The conductor swung them open, calling, "Coney Island!"

My heart pounded with excitement. Everyone in the dense crowd pushed through the gate to be first on the platform and down the stairs. I was suddenly afraid of being left behind, but Mama didn't relax her grip.

We were pushed through the gate and out onto the high platform looking down onto the street below. Stillwell Avenue was almost as crowded as the train. Mama pointed and said, "The Boardwalk is straight ahead."

Almost as soon as we were off the subway, I could smell the wonderful aroma from Nathan's Famous Hot Dogs. People crowded around, waving dollar bills to catch the servers' attention. Nathan's boasted hot dogs, hamburgers, milk shakes and orange drinks for a nickel.

The author, age 8, in 1932.

I breathed in the wonderful aromas that traveled on the soft breeze. The air had a salty tang, and combined with the smell of frying onions, it was almost more than I could bear. But I dutifully clutched the bag of bologna sandwiches I had been entrusted to hold and tried to ignore the sudden growling in my stomach.

We were carried along by the crowd. Mama said, "Everyone is heading toward the ocean. That's where the Boardwalk and all the rides are." Finally, the Boardwalk came into sight.

We stopped for a minute to get our bearings, and it was at that moment that my ear caught the wonderful sounds of Coney Island. I recognized the music coming from the merry-go-round. It was just like in the movies: a happy sound that

seemed to call people to join the fun atop the beautiful wooden horses that slid up and down on poles. I couldn't wait to actually see it. My feet did a little tap dance to the music.

The merry-go-round was momentarily forgotten when my ear caught a *clackety-clack* that I did not recognize. It seemed to come and go; when we were on the Boardwalk, I heard it again, this time accompanied by screams.

I looked up at Mama, a question poised on my lips, but held there by my promise to be good. Mama looked down and smiled gently. "That's the Cyclone," she said. "We'll walk to it so we can watch."

My friends had described the Cyclone as the scariest loop-the-loop in Coney Island, but nothing prepared me for the frightening clacking of the cars climbing the tracks to a high peak and the riders screaming in terror as they plunged to the bottom.

Still, it sounded like fun of the most exciting kind. Someday, I dreamed, I'd have enough money to go on any ride I wanted. For today, I'd memorize the rides I would save up for.

As we walked along, enjoying the view of the gentle waves, I wanted to stop and watch the sunbathers and swimmers. But Mama tugged me along, reminding me that I mustn't stare at people who should be ashamed because they were almost naked. The ladies wore black woolen bathing suits that showed most of their arms—and their knees! The fronts were cut so low that I blushed.

The men wore black tops with no sleeves (like Papa's undershirt), and the bottoms of their bathing suits didn't even reach their knees!

I sneaked a long-enough peek to find out why Mama thought ladies in black suits and men in black short pants and tops should be ashamed. I was embarrassed for them, but the bathers seemed not to notice. They didn't seem shy. In fact, I thought it would be nice to be so cool, playing in the sand and getting wet in the ocean. I faced forward as we walked, and Mama did not notice that my eyes were glued to the scene on the beach.

Children used tiny tin shovels to fill tin pails with sand. A man helped his little girl build a castle of sand. A family sat on a blanket, enjoying sandwiches and sipping drinks. Older boys threw a Spaldeen near the water's edge, falling into the waves with loud shouts of laughter. A man and a lady lay close together and kissed. I quickly looked away and felt my face grow hot. I wondered if that man and lady knew that everyone could see what they were doing.

Mama's voice interrupted my thoughts. "We're gonna see some freaks, and I don't want you saying anything to embarrass me, ya hear?"

With that warning, Mama and I gravitated toward a crowd before a high platform on which a man was shouting at the crowd: "Hurry! Hurry! Hurry! Step right up and see the most amazing, the most exciting sights of your life!" He held a large cone in front of his mouth and I realized that that was what made his voice so loud. I remembered seeing those cones in cartoons at the movies, but I hadn't realized until now why anyone would use one. A million questions roiled in my mind, but it would be better to save them.

"Ladies and gentlemen! Step closer and see one of the seven wonders of the universe! You see before you the bearded lady! She has the longest beard in the entire world! Watch out, ladies! That little mustache you see when you look into a mirror might someday look like this!"

Embarrassed titters arose in the crowd, and here and there, hands flew up to faces to check budding mustaches. I stared at the lady, open-mouthed with astonishment. She had a real beard, and it went down to her waist. I tried to get a closer look because I thought maybe she was really a man, but before I could decide, the barker bellowed, "Greater wonders await you inside. Adam the crocodile boy is swimming in his tank! Touch him! Talk to him! And then visit the fattest lady on the face of the earth—so fat she sits in an iron chair so it doesn't collapse!

"And believe it or not, Fannie the Fat Lady is married to the world's thinnest man, Stanley! Stanley is so thin that when he stands sideways,

Fannie can't find him! Imagine going to bed at night, ladies!" The crowd roared. "Come in and see for yourself! Don't be shy! For the price of one thin dime, you will be amazed and entertained! Step right up to the ticket master and hurry! There's very limited space, so hurry! You don't want to miss a minute of this once-in-a-lifetime show!"

I felt myself surging forward with the crowd. I tugged at Mama's hand and looked up at her to gauge whether there was a chance that we might go inside to see these amazing things. But Mama frowned and said, "Don't believe any of that stuff. They just want our money. Come on, let's go."

My disappointment was short-lived because of the wonderful aromas that wafted past my nose as we wandered up and down the narrow streets that connected the Boardwalk and Surf Avenue. We wound our way around pushcarts filled with steaming hot corn, frying onions, sausage and peppers, and cotton candy. The smells drove me to throw all caution to the winds and beg for a treat of hot corn. Mama looked down at me and said, "It's corn or the merry-go-round. You decide."

My stomach won. Mama nodded and asked for one ear of corn. I pointed to the ear I wanted and watched hungrily as the man pierced the largest ear of corn and drew it out of the steaming water. He carefully wrapped it in white paper and handed it to me with a smile. I ducked my head, suddenly shy, but took the corn eagerly. It was the most delicious, juiciest corn I had ever tasted. For years afterward, I remembered that corn and judged all other corn inferior to it. It was worth giving up the merry-go-round ride.

We found an empty bench along the rail of the Boardwalk where I nibbled my corn. The bologna sandwiches with lots of mustard were never so delicious. Mama said, "There's nothing like salt air to make you hungry."

My ear again caught the happy music of the merry-go-round. Now that I was full of good food, I thought longingly of the ride I wouldn't have—but then I remembered how delicious the corn was, and I was determined to be good.

"I guess you wish you could still go on that ride, huh?" Mama was reading my mind again.

I nodded mutely. "OK. I was gonna have a milk shake, but you can have your ride instead. But don't ask me for anything else, OK?"

I nodded solemnly, but then I could contain myself no longer. I jumped up and danced back and forth along the beach, chanting, "I'm gonna ride the merry-go-round!" over and over until a look from Mama quieted me.

The ride was everything I knew it would be. The loud, happy music made me want to dance and twirl, but I forced myself to stand quietly, watching and waiting for the ride to stop.

I carefully judged the merits of each horse as it passed. Some horses slid joyfully up and down on poles, looking like they could break loose and soar into the sky. Others seemed ready to leap forward at any second.

There were also beautiful benches that looked like thrones, but I dismissed the idea of sitting on one of them like some old lady.

Should I go on the pink-and-white horse with the flying mane and the wild eyes, or the white one with the big smile and the bells and ribbons around its neck? Would I be able to stay on when the horse moved up and down, or should I take a horse that didn't move up and down?

While I watched, I noticed some of the riders reach out and grab a ring from a metal arm. Then I saw the sign announcing a free ride if you could get the gold ring. I just *knew* I would be the one to get it.

When it was finally time for me to get on the ride, I watched Mama give the man the money. Clutching my ticket, I climbed up onto the platform and raced around to the other side where the horse of my dreams was waiting. Light

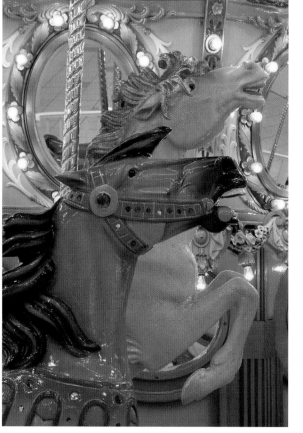

Photo courtesy Janice Tate

brown with darker brown spots, its ears pointed forward and its mouth was pink and laughing. Its black eyes looked at me as though ready to tell me a delicious secret. Pink and blue ribbons flew behind it, and its head was raised as though it would leap to the sky.

I was standing there, wondering how I could get up into the saddle, when I felt strong arms lift me. I found myself looking down at a very fat, sweaty man. I was too startled to be afraid of him, and besides, he laughed like Santa Claus. He said, "Let's strap you in good so you don't fall off. Now don't get down until I help you, OK?" I nodded.

Sure enough, the music started and the merry-go-round slowly picked up speed. It was like a beautiful, exciting dream—the music, the feel of the horse rising and falling, and the wind blowing my hair back with the horse's plaster mane. I couldn't reach out far enough to grab a ring, but I didn't mind. I waved at Mama each time I passed her. I was happy, and I was sure I looked just like Shirley Temple in *Little Miss Marker*.

All too soon, the day was over, and we trudged back to the BMT line. I was exhausted, and Mama didn't seem as happy as she had been that morning. As we rode toward home, I relived every moment and promised myself that someday I would be back. I'd save my money, and I'd ride every ride, and I'd eat cotton candy and hot dogs and as much corn on the cob as I could stuff into myself—and I wouldn't even bring lunch in a bag.

The rhythmic sound of the train wheels lulled me to sleep. As I drifted off, I heard Mama whisper in my ear, "Happy birthday, Honey." ❖

Fair of the Century

By Mario DeMarco

In the late 1930s, the World's Fair was in Flushing Meadows, N.Y., and our gang of boys, all members of the Buck Jones Rangers of America, decided it would be great to attend this momentous event. We especially looked forward to seeing one of the special attractions, Buck Jones' great horse, Silver.

Our biggest problem was money for railroad tickets and meals. The one-day excursion would cost about $20 per person. I got a job as a delivery-truck helper. Others sold newspapers, collected junk, washed cars and did other work to earn enough money.

We boarded the train and headed for the fair. It was a great thrill, riding the train. It took three hours to reach our destination. When we arrived, the giant white ball and the long pointed spike at the far end of the grounds—the Trylon and the Perisphere—were outstanding.

The war in Europe was still going strong during the World's Fair. That took a financial toll on the fair, as the exposition ended up about $18 million in the red. We saw some wondrous, futuristic ideas during our visit. Television was one of the chief attractions, and it drew great crowds. Another was the Firestone Tire and Rubber Co., which included a scale model of a farm on which tires were used for almost everything.

Europe was represented by the British Pavilion and the beautiful Italian Pavilion, which featured a statue of the Goddess of Rome with a giant waterfall. There were also exhibits from Australia and New Zealand.

After a while, we began to get hungry and tired. We took some time out to enjoy hot dogs and soda.

There have been other World's Fairs, but that exposition in New York has been regarded as one of the greatest. A week after our visit, we read in the newspaper that 44 million people had gone through the gates.

Attending this exhibition was a great experience. In the years since, we have seen some of the predictions and discoveries unveiled at the fair actually come to pass. Even so, we were a little disappointed that we never got to see Silver or Buck Jones! ❖

Symbol of the future at the World's Fair, 1939.

Summering in Atlantic City

By Linda Shapero

What do Miss America, Monopoly, high-diving horses, jitney service and Mr. Peanut all have in common? They all help define Atlantic City, N.J., the famous American city that many years ago was considered the nation's playground, comparable to Disneyland today. In fact, Atlantic City enjoyed its heyday during the 1930s and 1940s, and anyone who was anyone came there to see and be seen.

I grew up in South Jersey, and I remember how antsy I was, finishing up the last few days of school. They always seemed to drag on and on as I anticipated our annual summer excursion to the shore.

Nearly every year of my childhood and adolescence, we spent several weeks at the same boardinghouse, Sally's, in Atlantic City. It was owned by the friendliest landlady, who went out of her way to make everyone comfortable at their home away from home. Her guest house was large and rambling, like most of the others on State Street.

There was nothing like the smell of the salt air and the moisture that kissed your skin as you walked along.

We lived a mere 60 miles from the Jersey Shore, but when we packed the car and began our journey, we felt as though we were being transported to another world. The trip always seemed interminable because we were so anxious to get there.

Days at the Shore were slow-paced and relaxing, but still very exciting. We would get up early, have breakfast and then head out to the beach. We were not allowed to go in the water until at least an hour had passed after breakfast. The wait almost killed us, but we had fun in the meantime, running through the hot sand and building castles by the water's edge.

A few hours later, it would be time to eat. For lunch, we sometimes ate sandwiches (cream cheese and tomato, or sliced hard-boiled egg and tomato with mayo), fruit and drinks that my mother packed. Occasionally, we ate up on the Boardwalk, where we found a luncheonette or pizza parlor. The greasier the food, the better! Then it was back to the beach.

As we began to run out of steam, we paraded back to Sally's, where we rinsed off the sand at the outdoor shower around the back of the house. The walk back to the house always seemed so much longer than the walk to the beach. By that time, everyone was ready for a nap. The bright sun and saltwater did us in, and our naps usually lasted at least an hour or two.

After that, we dressed for the evening. That was our favorite time of day. Everything was more exciting and dramatic at night, and every business did its best to entice the crowds strolling by. However, as kids, we were interested in only one thing: the amusement-park rides. After dinner and a good, long walk down the Boardwalk (to properly digest our food), we were finally allowed to go to the amusement park, where we begged to go on as many rides as possible. When my father came down on the weekends after working all week, he always allowed us even more rides than my mother, so of course, we couldn't wait for the weekends and for dear old Dad to arrive.

I remember so vividly the cool breeziness of the nights at the shore. The sky above, lighted by millions of tiny stars, went on forever.

VIEW FROM MILLION DOLLAR PIER, SHOWING DENNIS, MARLBOROUGH-BLENHEIM. 61

CLARIDGE, BRIGHTON AND TRAYMORE HOTELS, ATLANTIC CITY, N. J.

Postcard courtesy Janice Tate

There was nothing like the smell of the salt air and the moisture that kissed your skin as you walked along, enjoying the sights and smells of the Boardwalk. It was even better when we stopped off for soft custard on a cone twirled in chocolate jimmies.

Sometimes we would sit on Sally's long, wraparound porch in the green rocking chairs that were scattered here and there. Some of the old-timers would sit and rock while they entertained one another with tales of younger days. We kids just liked to sit and observe the families walking by on State Street.

Sometimes my older sisters came with us. One of them, Myrna, had a boyfriend whose parents also vacationed in Atlantic City each summer. He worked at one of the concessions in the amusement park on the Boardwalk. That made him a celebrity in our eyes.

Occasionally we would go with them to Sonny's, a wonderful, old-fashioned ice-cream parlor near the house where his parents were staying. I always ordered a chocolate milk shake, which came in the biggest container I've ever seen. It was actually the size of a blender pitcher, but even as small as I was, I finished every luscious drop!

Another of our favorite adventures was going into Planter's Peanuts and shaking hands with Mr. Peanut. We were in awe of him, and we were always allowed to buy peanuts or some other treat to take home.

We also loved the salt-water taffy of all flavors and colors, and the molasses paddles covered in rich dark chocolate. How hard it was to make a decision in the taffy shop!

One of the best treats ever was going to Steel Pier to watch the shows and the main attraction, the high-diving horse. I only saw it once, but it was thrilling. How in the world did they ever coax the horses to dive?

The Miss America Pageant was another big attraction. I remember seeing many of the lovely contestants on the Boardwalk. Everyone pointed them out with a whisper.

Do you know what a "jitney" is? It's a very small vehicle that seats a few passengers. It was a popular way to avoid walking the Boardwalk. The driver sat behind you as you took in the sights and sounds of the Boardwalk. Jitneys were very popular. Pedestrians had to be careful if they didn't want to be run down by one.

Atlantic City has changed drastically. Gone are the diving horses and most of the other things that made visiting the city such an adventure when I was a youngster. But it will always remain one of the brightest memories of my childhood—a magical playground that offered fun and excitement for children of all ages. ❖

Opportunity of a Lifetime

By Fred Korotkin

The *Minneapolis Star* announced a contest in spring 1934 that really grabbed me. All-expenses-paid, three-day round-trips to the "Century of Progress" World's Fair in Chicago were to be awarded to the six newspaper carriers who signed up the most new subscribers. What an opportunity! I had never been out of town, to a summer camp, to work on a farm or for a vacation. And Chicago—the city of my dreams!

It had been founded as Fort Dearborn in 1833, was destroyed by fire in 1870, and observed its Century of Progress in 1933–1934. Even though I lived in Minneapolis, which had a sizable population, the thought of going to the big city of Chicago had terrific appeal.

The Great Depression was on. Our family could not afford to travel for pleasure or vacation. In fact, my brother and I were the wage earners in the household. Our father had deserted the family and sent no child support. Mother refused to apply for public welfare, so every cent I earned as a paper carrier went to support the family.

SKY RIDE, CHICAGO WORLD'S FAIR

Two years earlier, the Waterman Pen Co. had conducted a nationwide autograph contest. My entry was awarded an honorable mention, and the company announced that winning entries would be on exhibit at the fair. That was another reason why I wanted to go to the Chicago World's Fair.

The morning and evening *Tribune* and the *Sunday Journal* were the two established, dominant newspapers in Minneapolis then. They had the best features and news sources.

The *Minneapolis Star* was the newest daily newspaper in the city. In an effort to increase its circulation, the paper had frequent special

promotions to encourage carriers to sign up new subscribers. It wasn't easy to get them in 1934.

Most people had low-paying jobs, or were unemployed and could ill afford the luxury of a newspaper. Salaries were about $12 a week, and those who earned as much as $70 a month were considered well paid.

Even though a subscription cost only 45 cents a month, that small amount was a big consideration at the time. During the Depression, 45 cents could feed a family for a couple of days. In the Chicago World's Fair subscription promotion, new subscribers agreed to take the paper for three months, which added up to $1.35. That was a lot of money.

I delivered the newspaper in a poverty-stricken section of town where few people could afford home delivery of a newspaper. But poverty or no poverty, I was determined to go to Chicago!

How could I accomplish this?

On Saturdays and Sundays, during any free time I had, I went from door to door and pleaded with non-subscribers to sign up for the *Star* because I wanted to win a trip to Chicago. I must have been a fairly good salesman when I was a teenager, or else people were kind and wanted to help me win a trip. By the time the promotion ended, I had signed up almost 150 new subscribers. That made me one of the six carriers who signed up the most.

Hart Simonson, Gary Svobodny and I were the winning carriers who lived in North Minneapolis. The others lived in other neighborhoods, and I did not know them. Russell Peterson of the *Star's* bookkeeping department was our chaperone. Another teen, Harold Ogren, came along with our group. He wanted to go to the fair with others his age,

ENCHANTED ISLAND, CHICAGO WORLD'S FAIR

and he worked out some arrangement with the newspaper so that he could pay his own way and come along with us.

The trip to Chicago was my first trip away from home and my first trip on a train. In 1934, travel by train was the way to go—and oh, what fun!

The guys sat on the observation deck going and coming, and saw the farms, trees, lakes and rivers below. Along the way, some people waved to us as the train passed by. This was in the days before plane flights became commonplace.

In Chicago, the newspaper put us up in the Stevens Hotel in the city loop.

We were treated like royalty—swank beds, and two of us were put up in every room. For breakfast we were taken to the restaurant where we ordered orange juice, pancakes, cereal or whatever we wanted.

We toured as many exhibits and sideshows as time permitted and stopped for snacks or lunch whenever we got hungry. I saw the first burlesque show of my life there, and I didn't think it was anything special. Peterson and the others went to see a "live girlie show," which I passed up. They came out disappointed. What they saw were dressed-up mannequins instead of the living "girlies" they thought they'd see.

Now, these many years later, I have forgotten many of the details of the fair. On the other hand, some remain with me.

I realized that all good things must come to an end when I returned to Minneapolis. The exhibits and sideshows in Chicago have long been forgotten, but becoming acquainted with enjoyable classical music and delightful, healthy new foods have not. ❖

The Trianon

By Bob Langbein

The beautiful Trianon Ballroom, at 62nd and Cottage Grove on Chicago's south side, opened its doors in 1922. Patterned after the Palace of Versailles, it was built at a cost of $1.5 million by Andrew Karzas, who four years later built the Aragon on Chicago's north side. On Dec. 5, 1922, the ballroom opened with a benefit for the Children's Home and Aid Society. The ball netted $30,000 as Chicago society and theatrical figures jammed the ballroom.

The grand march was led by Mrs. Potter Palmer II. She was on the arm of General John J. Pershing, head of the

The grand staircase at the Trianon.

American expeditionary forces in France during World War I. Paul Whiteman and his band were brought in from New York for the dance at a cost of $25,000.

The next day, the Trianon Ballroom began its long career of public dancing. In this role, it played an important part in the lives of many Chicagoans. Quite often there was a meeting of Miss and Mr. Right. You could see it in their eyes as they danced to the music of "The Idol of the Airlanes," Jan Garber. Many a romance blossomed as he played his theme *My Dear*. Today, countless weddings can be traced to a "May I have this dance?" meeting at the Trianon.

In the warmth of the Trianon, people danced away their cares through Prohibition, a Depression, and a war. For an admission fee that most anyone could afford, the Trianon gave Chicagoans an atmosphere of unmatched elegance and romance.

The early 1920s to the mid-1940s were the days of Big Bands. Those closely associated with the Trianon included Jan Garber, Ted Weems and Lawrence Welk. In the mid-1940s, Welk had a girl singer with him named Jayne Walton. She was billed as "The Little Champagne Lady of Song."

The real glamour of the ballrooms—and the boom in the ballroom business—had its beginning with the opening in Chicago of the Trianon and Aragon. By the end of the '20s, they were the best-known ballrooms in America, probably because they so quickly saw the importance of radio, and through it, made themselves famous.

Hoping to emulate the success of the Trianon and Aragon, entrepreneurs erected similar ballrooms across the nation. During the next several years, Trianon ballrooms appeared in Oklahoma City, Cleveland, Los Angeles and Seattle, as well as in many other cities where they did not become quite so well known. The Aragon name was equally copied, with the best known to become established somewhat later in Santa Monica.

As the Big Band era passed, so did the crowds at the Trianon, and while management made efforts to attract suitable aggregations, it was never the same. When the Trianon closed in 1954, owner Andrew Karzas hosted a reunion of married couples who had met at the Trianon. He was happy to find there were no complaints.

A generation of Chicagoans were struck with nostalgic memories when, on Jan. 2, 1967, the Trianon fell to the blows of a wrecking ball. The dull thud of the crumbling walls sounded the finale for the once-magnificent dance palace, which had reverberated with the music of America's most famous bands. ❖

The Beat of the Street

Chapter Three

Maybe it didn't seem like a big deal to that fire chief back when our son was just a little tyke. But it sure was a big deal to Chad, and that made it a big deal to Janice and me.

We were living in Pasadena, Calif., in those days, and Chad was around the age of 3. Pasadena, of course, is both now and then known for the Tournament of Roses Parade that precedes the Rose Bowl game. We lived less than a block off the parade route near where it began on Orange Grove Boulevard.

It was a warm day on Jan. 1, as it often is in Southern California. The parade was over, and we had made our way to the park in central Pasadena that was the terminus of the parade where we could mingle with thousands of out-of-towners and get a closer look at floats, horses, and of course, fire engines.

Chad was always a big fan of the flame red engines and the men who so bravely rode upon them. He had his own toy fire truck and pushed it around the driveway of our home, going *"Vroom, Vroom!"* interminably.

As we wandered around the park, suddenly Chad pulled away from us, streaking toward a man in a dark blue uniform standing by, you guessed it, a bright red fire engine. Hurrying after him, all we could tell was that Chad was excitedly bubbling, *"Vroom, Vroom!"*

The chief was a kind man. I'm sure he had dealt with dozens, if not hundreds, of ebullient little boys in his career. I'm sure many

> *I realized that Chad was learning the beat of the street.*

wide-eyed youngsters became fireman recruits when some understanding officer lifted them up to the seat of their gleaming engine.

I never got the chief's name, but he sure made our little man's day. First, he pulled a red bandanna from somewhere and tied it around Chad's neck. Muscular arms lifted Chad from the ground to the dizzying height of the driver's seat. In imagination Chad took the fire truck through dozens of curves, pulling the wheel to the right and then back to the left, all the while screeching hot rubber in the corners of his mind.

The chief even let him pull the cord leading to the brass bell, and he clanged and clanged it in warning to the fantasy cars ahead of him to clear the way.

Then there was another little boy tugging at the chief's pants legs. Chad had to relinquish his high seat to a novice driver at least a couple of months his junior. He was comforted, however, when the chief introduced him to the department's dalmatian mascot.

I realized that Chad was learning the beat of the street, something I had never learned on the farm of my youth. His memory in those early days would be crowded with the hustle and bustle of the city. Did he grow up to become a fireman? No, today he is an accountant.

But that January day at the end of the Tournament of Roses Parade—along with memories of the parade of everyday life in the city—gave Chad a special appreciation for life along city sidewalks back in the Good Old Days.

—*Ken Tate*

Christmas in Chicago

By Roger J. Crotty

When I was a kid growing up in Chicago in the late 1930s, several things always happened that meant Christmas was right around the corner. A couple of weeks before Christmas, my mom would take my younger brother and me downtown on the Illinois Central train. It was an exciting journey. Once downtown, we went to the Fair Store. On the fifth or sixth floor, we walked up to a person who was dressed like a clown. We would tell him our ages, and an appropriate wrapped gift would come down a chute next to where we were standing. That was a great start to Christmas.

After that, we walked around for awhile, looked at the windows at Marshall Field's and visited the toy departments in all the stores (where my brother usually found some last-minute thing that he had to have and had neglected to mention to Santa Claus).

Dad used to worry, "Did we get them enough?" The answer was yes.

Speaking of Santa Claus, my brother and I always wondered why there were so many around. Every store had one. After much thought, we concluded that most of the ones we saw were his helpers. The way to distinguish the helpers from the real St. Nick was by the color of his outfit. The washed-out orange-looking ones were his helpers, and the real red one (usually at Marshall Field's) was really Santa Claus. This theory worked really well for us. The only trouble we had was one guy with broken glasses, strong-smelling breath and a black mustache that didn't go with his white whiskers.

After window shopping, it was time to go meet Dad at his South Dearborn office. We always stopped in the lobby so Mom could comb our hair

Tree in Town Square by Stevan Dohanos © 1948 SEPS: Licensed by Curtis Publishing

and straighten our clothing before we went up to meet Dad. Then we'd all go out to eat before going home, often to a place called Russell's Grill on the corner of Van Buren and State.

At home, the Lionel train boxes came out, each holding one of the cars or the engine for the Commodore Vanderbilt set. During the earliest years, Dad set up the tracks around the base of our Christmas tree. Later on, we screwed the tracks onto a couple of pieces of plywood painted with appropriate scenery. I can still see that train—and I remember the smell when we left the transformer on too long.

And of course, we trimmed our tree. There were three steps to trimming the tree: ornaments, lights and tinsel. With the first two, my brother and I helped out. But Mom was the real artist at hanging tinsel on a tree, so we watched that part. Our idea of how to hang tinsel was to stand about 5 feet from the tree and throw each strand at the tree.

The lights were also interesting because when one went out, the whole string went out. I volunteered to make sure the lights were all on because I liked the gold bulbs most of all and tried to get as many on the tree as I could.

Christmas Eve was the time when we exchanged gifts with our aunts, uncles, grandparents and cousins. The cousins used to put on some kind of play, with the parents as the attentive audience.

My main interest in life then was baseball; all the relatives knew I wanted to be a baseball player. Unfortunately, when it came time to buy me a present, they didn't remember I was left-handed. I unwrapped several right-handed gloves on those Christmas Eves.

When the Christmas Eve get-together wasn't

Old-time calendar illustration, House of White Birches nostalgia archives

at our house, we would have to drive home late at night. My brother and I always worried that Santa Claus would already be making his deliveries, and if he saw us still up, we would be out of luck.

One bittersweet memory of Christmas comes from one of the Christmas Eves when the extended family was gathered at our house. I was 7 or 8 years old, and being your typical Irish romantic, I was still a holdout in the arguments with the cynics in my class who had been saying for a long time that there was no Santa Claus.

During the course of the evening, the male cousins were into their usual roughhouse activities. At one point, we were behind the davenport in our living room. I saw my dad say something to an uncle, who immediately told us to "Get out from behind there and settle down."

Just before crawling out from behind the davenport, I saw something—and I knew why Dad had whispered. Underneath the davenport was the hiding place for the presents I was sure Santa Claus had in his sleigh (or big truck, in the event it didn't snow), which he was presently bringing to our neighborhood. When I went to bed that night, I cried a lot. Mom and Dad both came to talk to me, but I wouldn't tell them why I was crying. Childhood illusions die hard, and mine died harder than most.

Going to bed on Christmas Eve was a waste of time. We were up every hour on the hour, wondering if it was yet a respectable hour (anything after 5 a.m.) to get up and check under the tree. Being older and therefore the

The author (right) takes part in the annual family Christmas play with two cousins.

supervisor of the project, I made my brother check the clock a lot. Invariably, around 1 a.m., we would really fall asleep, and the next time we looked, it would be a legitimate time to get up.

Christmas morning. After all these years, one thing sticks out in my mind: I was never disappointed—and most often, I was overwhelmed. Mom says that Dad used to worry, "Did we get them enough?" The answer to that was always yes.

The other ritual from my childhood came after Christmas. One evening when the tree and presents were still in the living room, our front doorbell would ring, and there would be the neighborhood photographer, Galen, with about 50 pounds of photography equipment. It was time for the annual Christmas pictures. My brother and I would pose for what seemed like hours with our presents and with Mom and Dad.

Each pose was carefully orchestrated by the photographer. Part of the process involved putting cardboard visors on every lamp in the living room to focus all the candlepower available on the photo subjects. Mom has a great picture of me expressing my view of the evening with my hands, and at the same time, Dad's facial expression is expressing his view of my antics.

After Galen left, the Christmas season was officially over. The Lionel train set went back into the closet; all the boxing gloves, basketballs, mitts, games and toys went to our bedroom. Eventually, I got over finding out about Santa Claus. Fortunately, I will never get over the memories of Christmas in Chicago. ❖

Revisiting Sights and Smells

By Russ James

Have you ever returned to the place of your youth and found everything smaller and less pretentious than you remembered? Almost 60 years had passed when I returned to walk the streets of my youth. Nothing was the same, but as I paused, I could hear the sounds and sense the smells of those bygone days.

As a teenager during the late 1930s, my world consisted of several square blocks close to downtown Sacramento, Calif.

The streets were shaded by giant elms and lined with massive Victorian homes long since converted into cold-water flats—like our single room with its closetlike kitchen and shared bath across the hall. Time seemed endless then, filled with the long, hot days of summer and the sweat of breezeless nights.

The author pumps gas at 19 cents per gallon at the gas station where he worked in the early 1940s. Photo by Allan Willard.

Earthshaking rumbles and whistle blasts broke the stillness of the early morning hours as mile-long freights rolled slowly across town. I can still see the grim faces of homeless men, clutching their bedrolls as they huddled atop the boxcars, seemingly together in their quest for some unknown destination.

During the day, the sharp *clang, clang!* of a streetcar's bells could be heard above the clatter of its heavy wheels meshing in the narrow tracks. The trolley's single contact point with the power source above would spark and hiss, and many times render itself lifeless at the hands of fleet young lads.

I could almost hear again the pleading calls from pushcart vendors seeking rags and junk, and the *clip-clop* of horse-drawn fruit and vegetable wagons, all amid the sounds of early auto engines. I remembered the iceman, with bulging muscles beneath his water-soaked leather pads, handling large blocks of ice with ease. I recalled that musty smell of our small icebox with its drip tray and tin-lined ice compartment, and the woody taste of chipped ice from the back of the ice truck.

The buildings were gone, but I remembered the forbidding mystery of the corner tavern, with its strange sounds and darkness beyond the swinging doors. That ever-present exotic scent of smoky malt and warm grape juice seemed to fill the air just outside its entrance.

Down the street from the tavern was an Oriental laundry. I swear, I could still smell that aroma of starch and fried rice, and I could hear the strange language within.

Those unique smells in the corner grocery store came to mind: oiled and sawdust-covered floors, ground coffee, newly baked bread, freshly cut meat atop a butcher block.

A lot of my youth was spent around the corner, next to the alley behind our flat, at the brick-encased home of Engine Company No. 3. My eyes filled with mist that day as I viewed a "For Sale" sign on a degraded building with boarded window and doors. There was an air of silent dignity and strength about this structure. The crews stationed there always made me feel welcome as I shared their lore and wisdom. The invincible doors that reached high toward the second floor seldom offered a passerby a view of the mighty vehicles within.

On rare occasions, the unmistakable sound of the station's incoming message tape could be heard. People would pause with expectancy and gaze toward the muffled sounds of revving motors as the doors shuddered and slowly rose.

The shiny red engines, with sirens blaring and slickered firemen in command, would power into the street. The fading sounds of the speeding trucks and the lingering odor of diesel exhaust seemed incongruous with the tomblike silence of the empty firehouse.

I looked in vain for a trace of the corner service station where I had toiled while attending high school. I smiled as I remembered the odor of gasoline, grease, tires and inner tubes and that youthful feeling of achievement at 35 cents per hour.

Several blocks away, I paused near the corner where we spent endless summer nights

A quiet corner at the intersection of 19th and M Streets in Sacramento, near the station where the author worked in the early 1940s. Photo by Allan Willard.

sprawled beneath a dim streetlight. The smell of freshly cut grass, warm cement and burnt leaves seemed real. I tried to recall those mindless discussions of our youth—what did we talk about? I sensed the smell and taste of valley air when I pedaled toward home on those chilly nights, somewhat fearful of the quiet darkness.

As I left the old neighborhood, I could not forget a Sunday-morning game of alley football. A radio blared the news of some far-off island bombing attack, but our high school–age minds could not comprehend its significance.

I remembered most those eventful days when I could hear the distant newsboy's call "Extra! Extra!" As it grew louder and louder, my skin would tingle with apprehension. Little did I know that my sounds and smells of that era were evaporating, and that a generation's destiny had been cast.

Nothing would ever be the same again. ❖

84th Street

By Leola Hausser

*I*can still see myself sitting on the bottom step of the front porch at 1250 E. 84th St. in Cleveland, Ohio, and announcing to some neighborhood kids that this was our house, and we'd soon be moving in. Up to that time, we'd lived above Hausser's Home Bakery nearby, at the corner of 85th and Superior Avenue, where my father was head baker. We were just two children then—myself and my sister Ruth, three years younger—but my mother was expecting another child. That "child" turned out to be twins, Eileen and Kathleen, born after we moved into the house on 84th. When I was 7, my brother, Jimmy, arrived to complete our family. Father dubbed us "the hungry five," a take-off on a popular radio program, *Louis' Hungry Five*.

Everything in that neighborhood was within walking distance. Our world extended from 105th Street to 72nd Street. Why these boundaries? The Ezella at 72nd was one of the theaters, along with the Liberty at 105th, and the Superior in between, which were landmarks in our lives. We spent every Sunday afternoon in one of them, viewing Clara Bow, Tom Mix (with Tony the Wonder Horse) or Johnny Weismuller in *Tarzan of the Apes* and other silent films.

We watched as freshly baked bread came out of the big ovens on paddles.

At the corner of 84th, we loved Pehl's Candy Store, with its 5-cent Baby Ruth bars, 10-cent ice-cream cones, and penny grab bags, always with a prize at the bottom—usually a whistle that lasted for two beeps or a set of balloons that burst at once when blown up.

Across from Pehl's on the other corner was Klinger's Meat Market, where my mother often sent me for a half-pound of ground round steak for hamburgers or stew, which we ate often during those Depression years. Once, while chatting with Mr. Klinger, my mother turned to discover that Ruth, bored with looking at meat cuts, had pulled off all the leaves from his ferns in the front window.

My mother pulled her by the ear and whispered, "Just wait till you get home!"

Poelking's Grocery Store, next to Pehl's, was owned by corpulent, formidable-looking Mr. Poelking and his daughter, Mary, who was equally formidable. I dreaded shopping there because my mother would always say, "Be sure to shake the strawberry boxes. They always put the good berries on the top." I feared Mary Poelking's icy stare. The store was large and airy, and always smelled of fresh produce.

My earliest memory of Hausser's Home Bakery on 85th Street is of the morning my sister Ruth, then 2 years old, wailed and cried when her walker got stuck between two flour barrels. Later, when the five of us dropped in to watch my father at work, he'd line us up and squeeze marshmallow filling into our open mouths as we gagged and sputtered. We watched as freshly baked bread came out of the big ovens on paddles and was hoisted onto racks to be wheeled to the front of the store.

My Aunt Elsie was head clerk. When it came time to leave, Elsie would announce that since we'd been good girls, we could pick something to take along. Never a problem for me; I always picked a lady lock. They were large, and my mother would be embarrassed and say, "Why don't you pick something smaller?"

Hausser's Bakery, 8505 Superior Ave., Cleveland, Ohio.
Inset: The author's sister, Eileen, is the lady arranging cakes.

St. Thomas Aquinas School was near 96th and Superior, and all of us attended grammar school there. Across the way on Ansel Road stood Notre Dame Academy, where we four Hausser girls would later attend. Nearby East Boulevard was our Saturday-afternoon haven for roller skating. Its hills and curves left us red-faced and panting at the end of the afternoon as we unscrewed our clamp-on skates with keys and headed home.

I must not forget the 79th Street Library, so vital in our neighborhood. We took off for there every Friday afternoon after school let out. Our orange library cards entitled us to two books for two weeks.

Since one of my mother's house rules was no library books during the week, this was a regular weekend trip for us. Why no library books during the week? Well, according to my mother, we wouldn't get our homework done. But more importantly, we couldn't get our assigned household chores done with our "noses in a book."

Another reading rule was that nobody read your book until you'd finished it yourself. My mother dreaded settling arguments and was sure there'd be battles among all of us otherwise.

Our love of books started when Ruth and I were preschoolers and spent Sunday afternoons sitting, enthralled, as our father read *Heidi* to us, moving rhythmically back and forth in his old leather rocker. That loving image ends this glimpse of the old Cleveland where I grew up. ❖

Street Sounds

By Marty Toohey

The street sounds I heard during my childhood were part of the fabric of our neighborhood, a reflection of who we were and how we lived. The chant of the produce peddler was laced with an Old Country dialect as he cried out from a horse-drawn wagon. His horse pulled him, his wagon and probably most everything he owned along Fulton Avenue and throughout many neighborhoods in the Bronx, N.Y., eager not to miss even the smallest sale—a few plums, a melon or two, or on the best of days, a bagful of fruit or potatoes. He stopped at each apartment house, shouting, "Mel-oans! Juicy honeydew mel-oans!"

Our produce man sat unshaven under a weathered cap that already had seen many seasons in the 1930s, when I knew him. He wore clothes that had to get him through the day, come rain or shine, warm or cold, morning till night, as he eked out a living singing out the day's fruit and vegetable specials.

Tinkling chimes from the ice-cream man's two-wheeled wagon attracted throngs of anxious children.

The jelly-apple man, a short individual who wore a black bow tie and a well-trimmed mustache, offered candied apples from his pushcart. He announced his arrival with the same bellow every day: "Jelly app-ooos! Get your jelly app-ooos!" His appearance reminded neighbors of the toy groom that sits atop a wedding cake.

After dipping an apple on a stick into a pot of red candy liquid, he stood it upside down to form a flat surface of candy that hardened almost immediately—a highlight of the candy apple treat. Kids with red circles around their mouths had obviously enjoyed a "jelly app-ooo" that day.

"I cash clothes!" cried the vendor as he strolled the backyards of apartment houses and bought used clothing from anxious women who traded outdated apparel for small amounts of cash. He delivered his pronouncements in melodic fashion, allowing the words *cash* and *clothes* to run together, but communicating his meaning perfectly to all within listening range.

The "I cash clothes!" man was short and rotund, with a handlebar mustache that needed attention. He dressed in a threadbare suit that appeared to carry stains from his previous week's meals. The knot in his tie apparently never had been untied since the day it first graced his collar. He always carried a package, which everyone assumed contained used clothing, wrapped in heavy brown paper and held together with twine. He balanced it on his shoulder as he moved along. Few ever saw him open the package. Fewer women ever called to him from their upstairs windows; yet he continued to plod through backyards, shouting to the rooftops, "I cash clothes!" His chant echoed in distant backyards long after he had departed.

The cutlery man's stone wheel, attached to a leather strap and foot pedal, sent sparks into the air as it spun and sharpened the blades on housewives' carving knives. His right foot pumped up and down on the pedal like a pianist playing ragtime. We'd hold up newspaper sheets to catch the sparks and see if they caught fire, but they never did; and we marveled as

sparks flew at the cutlery man's face but never burned him.

His truck appeared homemade. The trailerlike body sat on the chassis of a truck that appeared to have been used for other purposes once upon a time. Made of a kind of dark bamboo, the truck was wide and fairly spacious inside. The cutlery man sat on a stool in the back, his foot pumping away. He didn't need a horn or a chant to announce his arrival. The screech of cold steel against stone told the neighborhood that he had arrived.

Tinkling chimes from the ice-cream man's two-wheeled wagon, powered by him as he pedaled the attached bicycle, attracted throngs of anxious children in search of frozen Popsicles, Fudgsicles, ice-cream pops and Dixie Cups that came with a flat wooden spoon. The circular lids on the Dixie Cups featured photographs of Hollywood stars. Some kids collected them.

Over time, ice-cream vendors drove trucks bearing names like Bungalow Bar and Good Humor. Some vendors conducted another business on the side, so to speak, from the privacy of their truck. They had their own betting business—lottery numbers based on the results of the day's horse races. Until then, we had been oblivious to his chime's dual message and the growing numbers of grown men who had developed a sudden taste for ice cream.

Trolley cars barreled along Boston Road and Webster Avenue accompanied by the clang of a large silver bell. It was an inviting sound when the weather was cold. Passengers bundled together, awaiting the trolley's arrival. I sometimes heard a trolley bell far off in the distance as I lay half-asleep. It only added to the comfort of my warm bed, away from the frigid air.

Garbage trucks detonated bursts of sounds night and day, depending on when they picked up trash. In addition to the racket of tin garbage cans against the truck's steel frame, trash collectors added the crash of the can when it was smashed against the frame of the truck to empty stubborn garbage that clung to the bottom; and the predictable sound that followed when the garbage can was slammed back down onto the sidewalk. Evidence of all this crashing and bashing was evident; not one of these cans carried the facial features it was born with, nor did the lids fit snugly.

The loneliest sound of the streets came from the Third Avenue el train late at night. I heard the plodding rhythm of the el's wheels as a solitary drumbeat: *thump-dee-dum*, *thump-dee-dum*. I had trouble believing that people actually rode the el at such a late hour, while everyone else was in bed. I imagined empty trains making round-trips to nowhere all night long. *Thump-dee-dum, thump-dee-dum*.

A comforting early morning sound, to my young mind, was made by the milkman as he made his deliveries from his horse-drawn wagon. I'd sometimes be awakened by the familiar, gentle *clippetty-clop* as the horse's hooves passed slowly over cobblestones.

As I lay in bed, I listened as glass milk bottles jangled lightly against the frame of the milkman's steel delivery basket. I heard his footsteps as he climbed the stairs in our hallway. He carried a steel basket of full milk bottles in each hand, up and down four flights of stairs, back and forth, floor to wagon and back again, until all the customers were served.

The milkman's horse was trained to proceed to the next apartment house on his route. A kerosene lamp swayed from the ceiling of the milk wagon as the horse plodded along. I owned a miniature lamp that hung from my toy Sheffield Farms milk wagon. When electric headlights replaced the kerosene lamps, I saw it as questionable progress.

Our neighborhood also was visited periodically by a one-man band. He wore a loud plaid jacket and a porkpie hat, just like performers in the movies, and played for coins thrown from windows overlooking the backyards.

"Throw him a few pennies, Martin. Be sure to wrap them in newspaper so they don't bounce and roll away," my mother would say.

The one-man–band man usually played a banjo, which by itself would have provided pleasant entertainment. But he enhanced his performance with clappers—metal noisemakers—attached to his shoes and to the fingers he used when he wasn't strumming his banjo. He also played a harmonica that was held by a brace around his neck, thus keeping his hands free to strum the banjo or click the clappers in accompaniment.

The one-man band would play until the coins stopped falling from windows above. Then he moved to the next backyard. We kids often followed him just for fun.

I grew up listening to these sounds of our neighborhood symphony, day and night. On occasion, when I spent a summer weekend with relatives "out in the country," nature's eerie silence and the crackle of crickets always kept me awake longer than usual. ❖

Facing page: *Scissors Curb-Side Service* by John Slobodnik © House of White Birches nostalgia archives

Beno's on Broadway

By Dale Geise

Beno's Department Store on Broadway in Council Bluffs, Iowa, was unlike any store I had ever seen. Where else would I ride in an elevator at age 10? I hadn't left Pottawattamie County except once to go to the rodeo in Sidney, 40 miles away. My mother had a dear old friend who sat on a stool and made the Beno elevator go up and down. While Mom renewed her friendship, I experienced the unsteady sensation of feeling the floor lift under me, and a little later, fall away. Carnival rides weren't much better.

Then there were the bewildering black things flying around Beno's ceiling. Metal canisters hurtled overhead on a spiderweb of cables and zipped down to sales tables where clerks stood waiting for them. I was fascinated to watch those shiny rockets—did they carry secret messages?

Later, I was disappointed to learn that they only held bills, checks and money. The cables converged on a balcony where a line of girls sat and emptied the cans, sending them flying back with receipts and change. All I needed was a burst of rocket flame coming from the back of the canisters to imagine that Flash Gordon was in charge of it all. But then, Ming the Merciless wouldn't be comfortable at Beno's.

Metal canisters hurtled overhead on a spiderweb of cables and zipped down to sales tables where clerks stood.

Down the block at Woolworth's and Kresge's were most of the five-and-ten-cent treasures in the world. The counters were heaped with little articles that seemed to me to appeal only to mothers on very tight budgets—or kids. I walked slowly with my mother and saw her examine and put back so many "needs" that cost but a few pennies. She sewed patches on our overalls and darned our socks over and over, so needles, thread, yarn and cardboard squares of buttons were always on her list.

I liked the more practical stuff—tin whistles, marbles, yo-yos, and very especially, the live baby box turtles with brightly painted shells. It was a dessert for the imagination to wander—looking, poking and inspecting—up one aisle and down another.

Only a few steps inside the door at Woolworth's stood the soda and sandwich fountain. Ladies sat on stools with their tuna fish sandwiches and thick crockery cups of coffee. The wall of mirrors behind the counter reflected lime green malted-milk mixers and pie slices stacked in glass cases. We passed on, only glancing at the white paper sheets taped to the mirrors and covered with watercolor ads for ice-cream sundaes dripping chocolate, nuts and maraschino

Council Bluffs, Iowa, circa 1946.

cherries. But seeing those and knowing they were out of reach of our pocketbooks left little hurt. Without question, these were items for some future time.

Before going home, Mom spent her grocery money at the People's Store. Christmas was the best time to be there. Rows of open wooden bins held mounds of nuts in the shell; striped ribbon hard candy; red raspberry shapes with soft, sweet centers; and old-fashioned drops— chocolate coating over a hard, white, sugary center. A stack of paper bags lay nearby, ready to be shoveled full. We did get special treats at Christmastime—certainly not enough to overwhelm us, but enough to make us deeply grateful for the last days of December.

Another thrill came as we climbed the wide steps to the second floor. Every step upward brought us closer to a toyland made of planks laid on cement blocks. Tin toys painted in bright colors and intricate details lined each rough shelf. Dolls were stacked higher than our heads, as well, though they barely earned a second look.

I loved the spring-wound army tanks and police motorcycles and bulldozers with real blades that could push dirt. One happy Christmas brought a Marx rubber-treaded tractor that clambered over the books we stacked in its path.

I returned more than once to a low shelf where a tin cowboy balanced on his rearing horse and twirled a wire lasso. Of the many toys I wished for at Christmas, that one came to our house, and though it has long since gone, it still makes me smile to think of the horse standing on his hind legs and tail, and the copper lasso spinning.

The People's Store stocked Kitty Clover potato chips. At what seemed like far too lengthy intervals, my brother, Dudley, and I shared a 25-cent bag. Kitty Clover will always hold first place among the potato chips of my life. My taste buds for grading special treats were not often called into action. Still, I could take a blindfold now, many years later, and pick Kitty Clover every time.

Council Bluffs had three movie theaters in the 1940s. The Strand seemed elegant because the front looked a bit like a castle. Maybe the glamour came from a real drugstore in the lobby with a front counter full of popcorn and candy. Across the street was the Liberty, where double features were common, and sometimes three shows in a row. All of them were "B" or lower pictures—mostly crime, cowboys, and some our parents might call "racy." If *Bad Girls in Prison* arrived in Council Bluffs, it probably would be shown at the Liberty.

A faded cardboard lobby ad saved from the old Broadway Theater hangs in my writing room. *Tahiti Honey* was showing with Simone Simon and Dennis O'Keefe, followed by *Man From Cheyenne* with Roy Rogers and Gabby Hayes. It was Bargain Day—"all seats 18 cents." The next evening would bring *Thumbs Up* with Brenda Joyce and Elsa Lanchester. Did audiences rush to the theater to find out why, as the ad stated, "She ignored a war-worried world to further a lifelong ambition"? Or was it the "Bank Award—$400"?

One unforgettable movie experience occurred when our school sent busloads of kids to Omaha, Neb., for Golden Spike Days. Omaha was and is a hub of the Union Pacific Railroad. Our exciting day in Omaha included a showing of the movie *Union Pacific* starring Joel McCrea. He was such a heroic figure, and he imprinted his wholesome bravery on my mind so clearly that about 20 years later, our second son would be named Doran Joel.

My mother and her sister Bess were embarrassed to buy bread in their younger married years. They baked every slice at home. But there came a time of a little relaxation and a bit of money when they could chatter happily over what to buy at the bakeries. Depending upon

Gabby Hayes, Roy Rogers and Sally Payne in Man From Cheyenne.

the year, there were three: Eve's, White's and Axelson's. What fun they had making their lists! If one went to town without the sister, of course she had to ponder just what Sister needed from the bakery. I always sent a silent wish for raisin bread with white frosting.

Passing up Broadway toward Canning Hill and home, I could see the Oaks Tavern, where my dad had taken me into the dark booths—a gloomy place for a child. But any fears were soon forgotten when the 25-cent special arrived—a thick, hot, beef sandwich covered in gravy.

Only one storefront remained that held any interest for kids. It was on the left side of our going-home route, resting among taverns and paint stores, and having the best sign of all: "Evan's Homemade Ice Cream." If the car even slowed going by there, I had high hopes. If the adults began discussing a stop, my chances improved. Then, a parking spot needed to appear quickly, or they would say "Oh, well" and drive on. They weren't aware of the roller coaster of hopes and fears going on in the backseat.

Behind the glass windows of Evan's, half the room seemed full of tubs of ice cream. The owner, in his round, white, flat-topped hat and white apron, always walked along behind the counter, smiling as we slowly searched each tub and read the labels. One side of the room was filled with pale lime-colored wooden booths where people sat and ate ice cream. What architect on his best day could devise a better plan than that?

I don't ever recall having Kitty Clover potato chips and Evan's Homemade Ice Cream on the same trip to Council Bluffs. If we had, that day would rest in a preferred spot on the mantelpiece of memory. ❖

The Street Cleaner

By Eileen Higgins Driscoll

Every neighborhood in Brooklyn had one. A street cleaner, that is. They were a necessity back in the 1930s. Cars were available, but most people in our middle-class neighborhood couldn't afford one. We grew up with public transportation. We walked, took a trolley car or train.

Why did we need street cleaners? I'll tell you about it.

Many enterprising businessmen came through our street with a horse and wagon. The milkman came every other day. His horse knew the route so well that he needed no direction.

The ragman was a colorful figure who rode on top of his horse-drawn wagon. A string of bells was strung up from one side of the wagon to the other. We could hear him coming down the street before he got to our house.

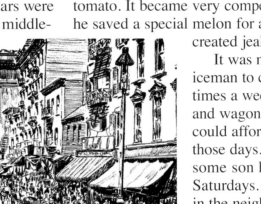

He yelled, "We buy old clothes!" His clothes looked like somebody else's throwaways. I don't know why we called him the ragman. He probably had a garage sale every week before anyone else ever had one; maybe he deserves credit for inventing them.

We also had a junk man with a horse and wagon. He was different from the ragman because he took big things. His wagon was loaded with chairs and beds and other assorted items. I suspect he may have had garage sales too.

Another interesting man who came through our streets sharpened things—scissors, knives and anything else that needed it. He was clean, neat and polite, and he guaranteed his work.

We can't forget the fruit-and-vegetable man. He had bells too, but he hardly needed to ring them. The housewives somehow knew his schedule and would lie in wait for him. They all wanted the biggest head of lettuce or the reddest tomato. It became very competitive. Sometimes he saved a special melon for a special lady. This created jealousy and gossip.

It was necessary for the iceman to come two or three times a week with his horse and wagon. Few families could afford a refrigerator in those days. His tall, handsome son helped him on Saturdays. All the young girls in the neighborhood were madly in love with the iceman's son. Me too.

Pony rides were exciting then. A pony and cart would attract mothers and children from the whole neighborhood. For a nominal fee, six children would be given a ride up and down the block amid happy yells and joyous laughter. Picture taking was important.

We had a modern bread and cake man. He had a truck.

But I've strayed from my discussion of the street cleaner. He had an oversize garbage pail on a pushcart with four wheels. The rest of his equipment consisted of a stiff broom and a large shovel.

His roundness almost matched his height. It would be difficult to determine his age. Singing, smiling and happy all the time, he went about his job, cleaning up after the horses. If there was no one to talk to, he managed to have a good conversation with himself.

I can't remember when he disappeared; probably the same time the horses did. Without knowing it, he was a part of the picture we grew up with in Brooklyn in the 1930s. I guess the loss of the street cleaner and horses was part of the "progress" they talk about. ❖

The Alley

By Frances Kalmett Dohr

We all fondly remember the Good Old Days, but some things about them were not so good. I was a city girl who longed to live in the country, with all that fresh air. At that time, the air in St. Louis was very bad because of all the coal-burning stoves and smoke from the many factories. We were still very active children, and we used the alley behind our home for a playground. The alley was also the route for many others who moved about by horse and wagon.

One was the garbage wagon into which the garbage man emptied garbage cans that housewives set out each week.

Sometimes, especially in summer, the alley could become very "fragrant" and was even infested with maggots. We never lingered there on garbage days.

Another wagon delivered coal, dumping it beside our gate in the alley. After work, Dad would shovel it into a wheelbarrow and roll it to the basement window, where he dumped it into the basement.

Every evening he would carry a bucket of coal upstairs from the basement, and every morning, the same bucket was filled with ashes and emptied into the open backyard ash pit, where we threw all our trash. The ash pit was built of wooden boards, just four sides 4 or 5 feet high.

Once a year, the ash-pit man would climb in with a shovel, shovel it all into his wheelbarrow, and roll it out to his wagon to haul it away. The rats would scatter when he got to the bottom. They never bothered him, and he was fearless.

In summer, the iceman came to the front of the house. Everyone had a sign in their window to let him know how much they wanted—10, 15, 20 or 25 pounds. He would cut a chunk of the proper size, put a burlap sack over his shoulder, lift the ice onto his shoulder with his big tongs and then carry the ice into the house. He dripped water all up the steps and across the kitchen before he put it in our icebox.

The author and Fido in 1925.

Then there was the ragman. He would buy old newspapers (which had to be tied in bundles first), small metal parts and old rags for pennies. Mom saved all the pennies, and at the end of the year, there was enough to go to the dime store and buy things.

The fire station was only a block away from our home. Until I was 3 years old, in 1924, the fire department used two beautiful, big, white horses to pull the fire wagon. I loved to watch them go by the house.

When we were older, the nice firemen showed us their dormitory where they lived above the firehouse and the pole they used to get down to go to a fire. In those days, the fire department used paper "ticker tape," which was imprinted as it ran through a small machine (the same thing that the stock market used). I don't know how it worked, but they got their calls from it and from the telephone.

But back to the alley … ours was paved with large, round, white cobblestones. They were very lumpy, but we played ball and other games out there. Once I wanted to be pitcher. I ended up being hit in the chest the first time around. It was then that I became an outfielder, as far away from the batted ball as I could get. Eventually the city paved the alley with cement. After that, many cars used the alley as a shortcut, and it became too dangerous to play there. But we were older by then and had other things to do.

The wagons were replaced by trucks, but they also were open and smelly. The worst thing on a summer day was to ride on a streetcar that was following a garbage truck. It happened to me in the 1940s—and it was not too pleasant.

One day when I was 3 years old, a group of us were playing in the alley when a man came by, selling socks and neckties. We teased him, calling, "Mr. Sticky, Mr. Stocky!" He made a spooky, mean face, stuck out his arms and said, "I'm going to get you!" We all headed for our yards, leaving the alley gate wide open. I was the smallest, so I was also last. The other kids ran up onto the porch and closed the door while I was still on the stairs. I thought the man was right behind me. I sobbed and screamed hysterically, and they finally let me in. The man had only been teasing us.

Years later, I worked in an office, and the man's wife, an older lady, worked there too. My mother had known his name and had met him years later, doing sales work. He was very nice. He taught us all a lesson that day. We never teased anyone again.

I don't have an alley now. I have a driveway where twice a week, I put my plastic bags for the waste truck. I love my G.E. refrigerator. I have a gas furnace. My old newspapers are recycled. But for some reason, when I look back, I still enjoy the Good Old Days, good and bad. ❖

Grab Bags

By Rose L. Korotkin

When I was a child, a penny was a small treasure. It bought something really swell—a grab bag. Back then, buying a 1-cent grab bag was a great adventure. We never knew what we would find in those magical little paper bags. They contained tons of candy. But there was also exciting variety. We got all kinds of stuff.

Grab bags were a great bargain. We got plenty for our money—and it was quantity that mattered, not quality. Oh, the marvelous surprises we found—giant sticks of Oh Boy gum, chunky Chocolate Soldiers and long-lasting suckers! Oh Boy gum was everybody's favorite. Just one section of the divided stick could be chewed for a whole week, if you were careful and kept the wad safely stuck under the kitchen table.

I was 6 years old when I was introduced to the wonderful world of grab bags. A classmate told me I had been missing out on some sweet deals.

I was timid and hesitant at first. I didn't know how to make the grocer understand what I wanted, and so I made a terrible mistake on my first transaction. I asked for a bag—and the grocer handed me an empty sack. It took me many days to get over my loss. Thereafter, I always remembered to utter the magic words "grab bag." Eventually I became a savvy customer. I comparison-shopped and took my business to the most generous grocery stores, where they sold the fattest, fullest grab bags.

How I relished those assortments of leftover gum, candies, Cracker Jacks and suckers! They weren't fresh and deluxe, but every piece was precious, the best-tasting morsels any kid could wish for.

Those were the Good Old Days, the sweetest days of my life! Hey, how about bringing back grab bags? ❖

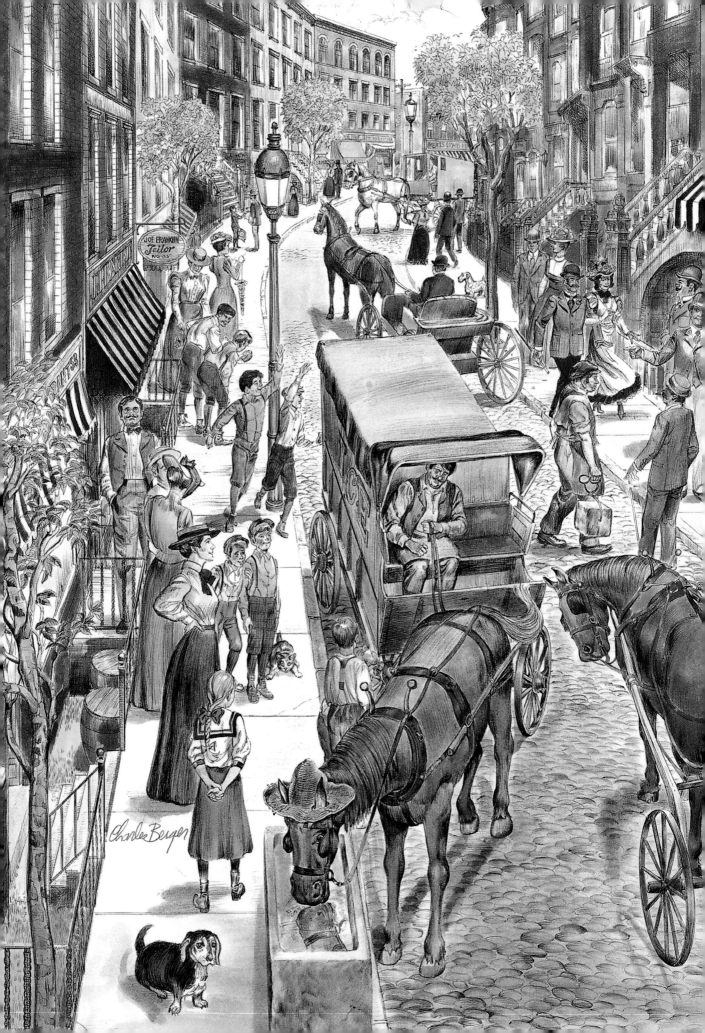

And Then the Frigidaire Stole Summer

By Patrick Fagan

Living through another sticky summer in the devil's boiler room—which Rand-McNally politely identifies as southwestern Indiana—prompted my kids to ask how I managed to survive before air-conditioning. I could think of only one possible explanation: the iceman of Carteret Street. Summers in New Jersey, where I grew up, were griddle-hot even by my Hoosier yardstick, and 1949 was no exception. As my brother, Jimmy, and I waited on the steps in front of Grandma Feeney's house, we regarded the heat as a temporary inconvenience, which her iceman, a ruddy-faced warrior only slightly smaller than a locomotive, would correct shortly after his arrival … if all went according to plan.

His name was Maloney—or Muldoon or Mulhern … the years have left some of my memory to guesswork—and his coming was announced moments later by his truck's peculiar rattle, which would remind you of the sound of pocket change tumbling in a clothes dryer.

"Thanks for looking after my truck, boys." The iceman's sandpaper voice startled us.

"Hot 'nuff for you, boys?" he rasped after hitting curbside. Sheepishly, I shook my head no, only to be overruled by Jimmy, three years my senior and considerably more accomplished in the beggar's art.

"Yes sir. Think heatstroke's got us," Jimmy said, pathetically. For emphasis, he wiped his brow with such dramatic exaggeration that neither Chaplin nor Barrymore could have added anything to it.

"Tell you what. Watch and see nobody helps 'imself to my ice, and when I'm done with your grandma, I'll see what I can do." Jimmy and I traded grins. If the man in the rubber apron noticed, he didn't let on. Instead, he leapt into the back of his truck and lifted the canvas to reveal a bed of ice so enormous that a family of penguins could have set up housekeeping.

Say what you will about Michelangelo and his David; nobody chiseled with more dexterity than Mr. Maloney. With a few deft thrusts of his ice pick, he separated a smooth, square block from its brothers.

The Ice Man Cometh by Charles Berger © House of White Birches nostalgia archives

Then, in one sweeping motion, he locked it in his tongs, tossed it over his shoulder and bounded up the stairs. He would be back within minutes, but it would seem like an eternity—not just because of the heat, but because the thought of standing sentry was horrifying. Our street corner may have been short of pubescent toughs, but when you're no bigger than a fire hydrant, you can never be too sure when your luck will run out.

As the minutes passed, melting ice taunted us as it dripped from the back of the truck, but we knew better than to set foot in the road. Our dad, Big Jim, made it clear that the street was off-limits. We devised a plan. I grabbed Jimmy's belt and anchored him to the sidewalk, while he stretched a cupped hand out from the curb. After catching his share, we reversed positions, but my diminutive size worked against me.

"Thanks for looking after my truck, boys." The iceman's sandpaper voice startled us. Being preoccupied, we didn't see him return. "Say, you wouldn't want the job permanent, would you?" He chipped off two waffle-size chunks of ice. "Watch my truck whenever I'm at your grandma's, and this is on me." The next thing you know, Jimmy and I held the ice cakes in our hands, numbing them momentarily, causing us to switch from left to right and back again to keep them from turning blue.

"Deal," said Jimmy. "Thanks." He elbowed me in the ribs to remind me of common courtesy—another parental dictate.

"Phwanks," I added without removing the prize from my mouth.

"Now, maybe I can get this old heap down the street before my load melts."

We kept up our end of the bargain, and the iceman kept up his. Then Grandma Feeney did the despicable, the unforgivable: She bought a Frigidaire—tall, white and totally electrified. The iceman was history. Summer had won the war.

Half a century has passed since the iceman made his last stop at Grandma's, and only two years have gone by since I had central air-conditioning installed in my

home. Still, even when Indiana summers prove intolerable, I'd be more than willing to trade my brand-new, high-efficiency, fully guaranteed monument to space-age cooling technology for one waffle of ice from the iceman. ❖

1942 Frigidaire ad, courtesy House of White Birches nostalgia archives

Home Deliveries

By Robert Pease

Even though I was a city kid, a horse-drawn wagon made bread deliveries to our house. The Manor Baking Co. delivered all over Kansas City in the 1930s using horse-drawn wagons built somewhat like today's mail trucks—enclosed, with shelves that held trays of white and wheat bread, cakes, doughnuts, even cookies—but no muffins or bagels.

We kids gathered at curbside and talked to the nags as they waited patiently for the delivery-man to return, grab up the reins, release the foot brake and continue *clop-clopping* up the street to the next customer's house. We stroked the horses' velvety noses, studied their big, sad eyes, and said things like "Nice horsie" and "Good boy, good boy" as they stomped nervously and shook their manes.

We figured that the Manor man had just about the best job a person could hope for, unless it was the ice-cream man, who drove his little truck along our street almost every afternoon in summer. His merry jingle played over and over so we'd have time to cadge a nickel or maybe even a dime from our moms to buy a cooling treat.

Nickels were scarce, and we were often refused. However, the camaraderie of hard times fostered a spirit of sharing. It was a good investment to give bites to those from whom you would be asking bites later.

Favorite treats included Drumsticks, Fudgsicles and the double-dip cone. But more often than not, we opted for Popsicles. They had two halves on tongue-depressor sticks and could be divided, so two kids could enjoy one nickel's worth. My favorite was cherry, but I was also quite happy with donations of lime, orange and grape, so long as I got a half from somebody; it was a debt we could not fail to repay.

When our families began buying refrigerators to replace iceboxes, some of us tried making our own Popsicles, freezing Kool-Aid in ice-cube trays with toothpicks angled through them. They weren't great, but they were better than nothing—except that our moms complained about the cost (and during the war, the scarcity) of the sugar needed to sweeten the Kool-Aid.

When there was no "loose change" for the ice-cream man, we could fall back on the iceman, who came twice a week in summer. He'd pull up in his City Ice truck, go around and toss aside the tarpaulin in back, revealing 100- and 200-pound slabs of clear ice, some of the insulating sawdust clinging to them. He used an ice pick to separate blocks of 25 or 50 pounds, depending on the color of the card the customers displayed in their front windows. Then he hooked the block with his big steel tongs and heaved it onto his shoulder, which was protected by a flap of burlap, and toted the ice to the icebox on the back porch.

We gathered around as he chipped the ice with his pick. Then, as he disappeared up the driveway, we'd grab up the heftiest slivers. When he returned, if we hadn't found sufficient pieces, he'd chop a few more for us. Then he'd pull the tarp back in place, jump into the driver's seat and rumble off up the street while we sat on the steps and sucked our ice just like Popsicles. It was a real treat on a hot summer afternoon—and well worth the price. ❖

My Kansas City Home

By Helen Patton Gray

*I*t was June 30, 1930, the middle of the year as well as the middle of the Great Depression, when my parents, Clarence and Minnie Patton, brought me home from St. Luke's Hospital in Kansas City, Mo. My two older brothers, Richard and Jack, could hardly believe that the little sister they had prayed for had finally arrived. I would live in our small bungalow on a steep hill for the next 22 years as the baby of the family. I was never told that we were "poor." In those days, families were lucky to have their own home with indoor plumbing and three bedrooms.

One of our bedrooms was in the front of the house. My bedroom, a walk-through off the kitchen, led to the third, which my brothers shared. The closet space was adequate, though not generous.

There was a back porch off the tiny kitchen where Mom did the laundry early every Monday morning. The Maytag wringer washer stood ready. One of its rinsing tubs had bluing added to bring out colors. By noon, the clothing and linens would be on the clothesline, ready to sway in the breezy sunshine.

The author's mother, brothers Dick and Jack, and the author in 1934.

Tuesdays were ironing days. Some items were starched and had to be sprinkled. Dad's shirt collars and cuffs, doilies and sometimes table linens received special attention. This was long before the "wash and wear" era.

Other "mom chores" were airing throw rugs, dusting furniture, mending socks and scrubbing floors. Even so, she always made time to turn on the radio in the afternoons so she wouldn't miss an episode of *Our Gal Sunday*.

My big brothers cut the lawn with a hand mower. They also had regular customers for lawn care, and they earned about 25 cents per hour.

Grandma Patton liked to sit with me on our front-porch swing, telling me stories about how my brothers had prayed for a baby sister. That was hard to believe as I grew older and became the "teased one." But that was the way it was in those days in our neighborhood. Little sisters were always teased.

Grandma Patton worked part time as a housekeeper and baby sitter for several families in town, and she lived with us for part of the time.

When I was 4 years old, she gave me a beautiful navy blue wool cape with a red lining. It had red buttons shaped like cherries. I was so proud of it! No one I knew had such a nice piece in her wardrobe. When I outgrew it, it was passed on to another family member.

After school, it was playtime with the neighbor kids. Our next-door boys, Jackie and Ralph, loved to play rubber guns with my brothers using homemade weapons and ammo. After dark, there was usually a game of hide-and-seek, or we enjoyed story time with the master storyteller, my brother Jack. He sat on the front steps with all the neighborhood kids perched around him, anxious to hear his ghost stories.

Those same steps served as our make-believe "school." The one who had drawn the longest straw got to be the teacher. She picked up a small stone and held it concealed in her hand, behind her back.

"Students" began class by sitting on the bottom step. Then, with fists closed tight, the teacher reached out her hands to each student. When the student chose the hand with the rock in it, he or she advanced to the next step. The first student to reach the top step became the new teacher, and a new round began.

I live in Wisconsin now, and I sometimes miss twilight in Kansas City, where the katydids and locusts grind out their "music." It's not very melodic, and eventually it becomes boring. But on a recent visit back home, I listened to their serenade again and realized how long it had been since I heard it.

Then the "lightning bugs" started to flicker, and my imagination ushered me way back to childhood days, when we also had ample swarms of mosquitoes and the little red bugs in the grass that we called "chiggers." They are actually a type of little red tick, and they can

The author leaving for a date in 1949.

get under the skin. We used home remedies like kerosene on the bites, so we "paid no nevermind" when they came around.

I walked with my brothers one mile up and down hills to and from St. Louis School each day. Mom packed our lunches, wrapping them in past issues of *The Kansas City Star* newspaper. We got metal lunch boxes eventually, and even Thermos bottles. It was the boys' job to carry them. After they graduated from grammar school, I was on my own to carry things back and forth. By then, however, I had my first bike.

I will never forget the day—I was 10—when I learned that my brother Jack had joined the Navy and would be off to basic training. Dick, my older brother, had been blinded in his right eye in an accident, so he was 4F. But he wanted so much to join! Later, he was reclassified and did leave home for the Army.

Several other homes on our block had service star flags in their windows, just as we did. The flags were reminders to write to the boys and pray for their safe return. Luckily, all of the boys came back years later, grown up. But soon after they returned, they married—and then they were gone once more.

The neighborhood seemed deserted in those years, with only "aging" people living on Montgall Avenue. I had graduated from high school by then, and I went to work for the government. Eventually I met my husband-to-be, who was in the Army at the time.

Years went by, and the city expanded. Prospect Avenue, the next street over, became a freeway. The homes on our street were bought out and all the residents were relocated.

The Depression years were slim on money, but they left us rich in fond memories of the Good Old Days of close families and friendly neighborhoods. Most of us wouldn't wish for times exactly like those, but they make good stories to tell our family and friends. ❖

Scents of the Past

By Marie L. Franks

The adage "Follow your nose" has more meaning than just the traditional reference to heading in the right direction. Smells, odors and aromas are so tied to our emotions that a quick whiff of vanilla can recall memories of Mom's chocolate chip cookies and the warm, comforting feelings of home and love associated with that particular treat. I can follow certain smells right back to my childhood.

I grew up in the 1950s in an Italian neighborhood in Cleveland, Ohio. Hardworking immigrants—farmers, masons and laborers from the region of Abruzzi near the Adriatic coastline on the Italian peninsula—lived in sturdy old one- and two-family houses with small front yards.

Photo courtesy Janice Tate

Few families had cars. Husbands and fathers walked to work or took the bus; children hiked up the hill to school. Moms and wives worked at home. Windows and doors stayed open in spring and summer, and the air was fragrant with the smell of simmering tomato sauce and the scents of fresh basil and garlic. In late summer and early fall, you could smell the grapes fermenting for Mrs. Fusco's wine.

The aroma of incense drifted from the Catholic church, which sat majestically at the top of the hill. Mass was the traditional Latin Mass, with pomp, ceremony and incense. I knew the Mass in Latin from beginning to end.

To this day, the smell of incense transports me back to the days when nuns ruled, and the school day started with Mass and ended with prayer. I still don't really like the English Mass, because it has none of the mystery of the Latin Mass, and incense is not used so often now. Schoolchildren and pious little grandmas dressed in traditional black attended daily Mass, but everyone celebrated Mass on Sunday. Afterward, my father and most of the neighborhood would stop at the Italian store to buy fresh pasta, Parmigiano Reggiano and olives.

On Sunday mornings, even in the coldest weather, the store's old wooden and glass door stayed opened. The enticing, pungent aroma emanating from within beckoned the neighbors returning from church. The floor and walls were wooden, and the scents of cheese, pasta and olives penetrated everything, including the paper sacks used to carry purchases home.

Big barrels of black Lugano and purple, wrinkled Gaeta olives gleamed and glistened in front of the deli counter. Their smell called to me as soon as I walked in the door. You could scoop the quantity you wanted into white paper containers similar to those now used for Chinese takeout. I am not sure how sanitary that was, but it was certainly effective. Could you leave without buying a quart?

The pasta was fresh and tender, usually made by the wife of the shop owner. The dough was hand-mixed on a big floured board, then rolled flat and cut. It was a time-consuming process, completed with great care. Everyone that bought it was a "Paisano" from the same town in Italy, someone who "came over on the same boat," a cousin, or at the very least, a neighbor.

Neighbors lingered to catch up on the news before continuing home to spend the rest of the day with family. Everyone had lots of family. In the early 1950s, we had at least 20 relatives within walking distance of our home.

The week passed quickly, aided by the rituals prescribed by church and school: Mass on Sunday followed by family visits, daily Mass and prayer with school wedged in between, and finally, Friday! Long before "TGIF," Italian neighborhoods had special Friday traditions.

Friday was a day of fasting and penance in memory of our Lord's death. In the 1950s,

Catholics followed the tradition of previous generations and did not eat meat on Fridays.

We would fast all day. Then, at about 11:30 on Friday night, the neighborhood would come alive. In almost any weather, you saw most of the neighbors, walking in small groups, lingering to talk, and heading for Orlando's Bakery. The Orlando brothers baked the bread for the weekend on Friday nights.

The aroma of incense drifted from the Catholic church.

Smart and resourceful merchants, they also opened the shop at about 11 p.m. The smell of baking bread drew us to the bakery.

While neighbors might linger on the way to the bakery, they hurried home with their hot, fresh Italian bread to break the fast. Of course, some pepperoni and provolone would accompany the feast, eaten with hunks of the fresh bread.

Pepperoni and provolone were never used on top of pizza, at least not the pizza my mother made. Her pizza was square, with a thick crust covered with a thin layer of sauce and onions, and lightly sprinkled with grated Pecorino Romano.

To this day, the smell of onions and tomatoes seasoned with oregano brings back memories of my childhood and the anticipation of the holiday or other special event that required the baking of Mom's pizza.

Predictably, the old neighborhood is different now. The children of the immigrants moved to the suburbs. Orlando's grew, prospered and moved to a large, new facility in another neighborhood. The church still stands, and Mass, in English, is said once a week. The school building is still used, but for other programs. People from other backgrounds and countries live in the neighborhood. New special and different smells waft out from the little ma-and-pa store on the corner.

Odors, aromas and smells have the power to take us places we haven't been in a while—places where things seemed simpler, desires could be met with a taste of something familiar, and security meant Mom and Dad. I sometimes wonder: If I travel back to the old neighborhood at midnight on Friday, will I smell bread baking? ❖

City Sidewalks

By Margaret Piipke

It was 1945, the first Christmas after the end of World War II. I was 8 years old, and my brother, Chester, would reach his 10th birthday on Dec. 8. The day after Thanksgiving, we were going to ride a bus to downtown Pittsburgh. It was time to see all the decorations at the department stores. Boggs and Buhls, Hornes, Gimbels and Kaufman's department stores had large display windows on each side of the front doors. These windows were covered with ugly drapes for a week before the magic day. Behind them, workers were turning them into a Christmas wonderland.

My brother and I were up and dressed before daylight, wondering what we would see once we arrived downtown. We had to be quiet since my father worked at night and was now asleep. We stepped softly down the hall to my parents' room, whispering to each other to open the door. Finally Chester reached for the knob. But before he could open it, Mother came out. She was dressed too.

She made us eat breakfast before we left the house. The bus stop was a mile away, but we didn't mind the walk. We could hardly hold in our excitement as we skipped along the sidewalk. It was an event for other people also. The streets were crowded with mothers and kids. We all wanted to see the magic that was Christmas.

At 9 o'clock, as if with the wave of a magic wand, the drapes came off the department store windows. Suddenly there were a million things to see. One window showed the inside of Santa's workshop, where his elves worked on toys for delivery on Christmas Eve. All of them had moving parts, and some even sang.

Main Street at Christmas by Peter Helck

One window showed a family decorating the tree by a fireplace. Another featured ice skaters on a frozen country pond. And at yet another, we saw carolers dressed in turn-of-the-century clothes, standing outside a window, singing.

We raced from window to window, trying to see everything at once. The windows closer to the doors were the ones where the most was going on. We would start at one end of the window, trying to find something the other had missed. We called out to each other, telling what we were seeing.

Adding to the festive atmosphere, vendors stood on the street corners, selling roasted chestnuts, mistletoe and large pinecones.

The highlight of the day was not talking to Santa—though we did—but having lunch at Kaufman's. The restaurant we picked was on the balcony of the second floor, and we had a table by the railing, where we could look down to the first floor and watch the people shopping.

Finally, at 6 o'clock, we started for home. It seemed to take longer going home than it had coming in the morning. Riding on the bus, we fell asleep leaning against Mother, me on one side of her and Chester on the other. When we reached our stop, we walked quietly beside Mother back to the house. We were two tired kids, but what a great day we had had!

It was the beginning of the Christmas season, and we still had lots to do. We had to write our letters to Santa and pick out a tree.

For the next few days, we worked on our letters. After many drafts, they were finished. We carried them to the mailbox.

Of all the holidays for which Mother did special things, Christmas was the one she loved best. She worked on her knitting all year, whenever she had a free moment. After the evening meal, once we were in bed, she would sit in the living room in an old wingback chair near the fireplace. It was her favorite place to knit and listen to the radio.

Picking up her needles and yarn, she would work on her latest project—a sweater, mittens, a scarf or a hat for one of us kids or Daddy. When it was finished, Mother put it away until she placed it under the tree to be opened Christmas morning.

Mother baked and cooked for days in preparation for Christmas, making pumpkin pies, a mincemeat pie for my father, candy and lots of cookies. Sometimes she let us help decorate the cookies. She also made rolls and her great Swedish tea ring and bread, but she made that all the time.

The year 1945 was also special because my oldest brother, Paul, was coming home for Christmas. He had been in the Army Air Corps, and it had been two years since we had seen him.

Each stocking was filled with an apple, an orange, a candy cane, a coloring book and a box of crayons.

After supper on Christmas Eve, I was getting worried because it had started to snow and Paul had not arrived. Our baths were over, and we had set the milk and cookies out for Santa, eating a few ourselves.

The time was going so slowly. Past 8 o'clock, and still no big brother. Why was he so late? Mother said we could wait for him even though it was past our bedtime. But I was having trouble keeping my eyes open. I lay down on the sofa to wait, figuring I might as well be comfortable while I waited; I wasn't tired or anything.

On Christmas morning, I woke in my own bed. Chester ran into my room with his stocking. Mine was hanging on the bedpost, as it had on all the Christmases before. Each stocking was filled with an apple, an orange, a candy cane, a coloring book and a box of crayons.

We hurried down the stairs. Mother stood at the bottom to stop us from running into the living room. We had to eat breakfast before we could see what Santa had brought us. As she led us to the kitchen, we turned to look into the living room, but the double doors were shut. Sitting at the table was Paul, calmly eating. He had arrived after we fell asleep, and it was he who had carried us up to bed. We ran to him and gave each other hugs and kisses.

For years thereafter, I believed he had come with Santa. How else could he have gotten home when there was snow on the ground?

Once breakfast was over, we walked into the living room. The tree was trimmed, and under it was an American Flyer sled for me and a Lionel train for Chester, both from our older brother.

Mother had been up before daybreak, preparing the 20-pound turkey. She saved all the pieces of bread in a large covered dishpan that stood on the icebox on the back porch. She stuffed the neck and inside cavity with the bread stuffing. It would cook for hours, sending the smell through the house. My father's parents came at noon, bringing my sister. She worked in the city and lived with them.

At 2 o'clock we sat down to eat. The table was loaded with turkey, mashed potatoes, gravy with giblets, candied sweet potatoes, lima beans, cranberry sauce, a dish of celery stuffed with cream cheese and peanut butter, and a Jell-O salad. There was a relish dish of gherkins, sweet pickles, green and black olives, and spiced apples, and there was pie for dessert.

After dinner we were permitted to take the sled outside to try it out. We rode the sled down the hill and then ran back up, pulling it behind us. We made many trips up and down that hill until we finally had to come inside, numb from the cold. But after a few minutes in front of the stove, we were as warm as toast and ready to go again.

There were other winters and other Christmases, but the year I was 8 years old is the one I remember best.

I live in the South now, and there are no department stores to go to, only malls. There are no large windows decorated for Christmas. It's a little sad that the stores put Christmas things out in the middle of September; it is for me, anyway. I do take my granddaughter to see what new toys there are the Friday after Thanksgiving, but there is no surprise; by then, she has seen them advertised extensively on television for months.

For me, the magic that was Christmas long ago is gone. ❖

The Organ-Grinder

By Dorothy Anna Birkholz

Thinking about the old days, I remember the organ-grinders who came around our Chicago neighborhood. It was 1923, and I was 5. A man would come walking down the street, playing music on a small hand organ that was housed in a wooden box about as big as an apple crate.

A stick like a broom handle protruded from the bottom, and the organ-grinder balanced the box on it when he stopped to play the organ by turning the organ's handle. The ends of a wide leather strap were attached to each side of the box, and he wore the strap around his shoulders to help hold the organ up as he walked.

The music was nice, but the best part was the little monkey that sat on the organ-grinder's shoulder. The monkey was about a foot tall. It wore a little red jacket and red cap, and it carried a small tin cup. When the organ-grinder finished playing, he would let the monkey go among the people who were listening so they could drop coins into his cup. When they did, the monkey would tip his cap and return to the organ-grinder. My mother always gave me a few pennies for the organ-grinder, and I was so excited when the monkey took them from me.

Sometimes a gypsy woman would come down the street with a big organ that looked like a small spinet piano. It had two wheels at one end and a handle at the other so she could roll it along like a wheelbarrow. She turned another handle on the back to play the music. It was nice to listen to, but we children all preferred the man and his little monkey. ❖

The Tinker Man

By Eugene D. Atlas

The first sign of spring in Mariners Harbor was not the bloom of crocuses or daffodils. The gardens of our shipyard town in the early 1920s were too valuable for flowers; they were reserved for vegetables. Our first sign of spring was the merry clang of the tinker man's bell as he energetically swung up and down our residential streets.

The tinker man always seemed to be a short, stocky Italian immigrant who cheerfully sang out in garbled English, "Pots, pans, scissors and knives!" He had come to repair and sharpen all kitchen utensils.

One tinker man came to our town every spring. His pants were baggy and patched on both knees. He always wore a heavy, colorful plaid shirt and a bright scarf, tied around his neck in a huge bow. His felt hat had a high crown and a floppy rim, which he pulled down over his face when he was working. He always needed a shave, but his bright teeth and sudden smile made up for his scruffiness.

My eyes were glued on his hands as they shifted from tool to tool with never an interruption or doubt.

On his back he carried a heavy wooden stand on which was mounted a hand-operated grinding wheel. Hanging from the stand, rows of tools jingled, adding to the clamor of his brass bell. Housewives brought out whatever needed repairing or sharpening, and the tinker man set up shop right there on the sidewalk.

The first tinker man who hit our streets each spring did a great business, if not a gold mine. All the housewives were waiting anxiously for him. Most pots in those days were made of thin aluminum or enamelware. If the housewife was careless and the pot overheated, the flame burnt a hole in the bottom of it.

Mom cooked all our meals in the back of our store. Inevitably, she burned through the bottoms of many pots, trying to wait on customers while preparing meals. She never thought of having any of her three sons help in the kitchen. That might distract us from doing homework—that is, if we were not working in the store.

The aroma and taste of burnt vegetables was so normal in our home that forever after, we three sons nostalgically missed this extra flavor never found in our wives' cooking.

When the smell of burning vegetables flooded the rear of the store, one of us boys would finally jump up, turn off the offending gas flame and yell, "Hey, Mom, the vegetables are burnt again!" And then we'd sit down and wait for Mom to clean up.

That was the way we were brought up. Mom was there to take care of all problems. While we boys always worked in the store, somehow we never helped in the kitchen. It was never expected and never done. Mom never complained or suggested that maybe one of us might at least lower the flame or scrub the pot.

By the time I was 8 or 10 years old, the tinker man's bell was an exciting call to me. I already loved to watch men work with tools—any kind of tools. I would stand by his side, enraptured by the cool confidence and dexterity with which he used his tools. My eyes were glued on his hands as they shifted from tool to tool with never an interruption or doubt.

This itinerant working-man's dexterity and competence provided another role model for me. My father seemed weak and indecisive compared to this poor handyman and all those big, strong, confident shipyard men. Unlike them, my father never lifted anything heavier than a box of shirts—and he had no ability with tools.

Each spring, when the tinker man showed up, I pulled him around the corner to the front of our store and happily brought him all our pots with holes. The long winter had seen the ruin of most of our pots. I watched him carefully as he repaired each pot and pan. I was determined that someday I, too, would be able to repair a pot.

My ambition in life was to become a man of tools like the tinker man, or to wear overalls and smell of grease and sweat like the big shipbuilding men who came into our store and bought those handsome work gloves and heavy work pants. Forgetting the college I was heading for, I vowed that someday I would be one of them.

He repaired small holes in pots by inserting a metal plug in the hole and hammering it flat on a small anvil mounted on the stand. The tinker man then heated the plug with a small torch until it flowed smooth, and finished the job on the grinding wheels. This always left a ring to that was difficult to scrub clean.

Larger holes required two washers, connected by a pin, and then the soft, melted metal. A dam—called a tinker's dam—was placed around the hole in order to prevent the molten metal from flowing away from the hole. This dam was only temporary. If it broke during the repair, the job would have to be done over. This led to the expression "not worth a tinker's dam."

The problem was that these plugs were composed of an aluminum alloy that melted at a fairly low temperature. The plugs never lasted long; even normal use would remelt them on the stove. But no utensil was ever thrown out. Everything was fixed and repaired.

Because the cost of each repair was so small, the tinker man had to be fast and dexterous to

A tinker's torch.

make a living. All prices for repairs were greeted by loud screeches of "Robber!" in English, Italian or Polish.

The tinker man never argued. He might not have understood, but the message was clear. He would just stand there impassively, one well-worn hand outstretched.

Mom never bargained with the tinker man. Maybe she did not have time to haggle, or maybe she had sympathy for the hard way in which he made a living.

His bell sounded even jauntier after he pocketed the coins and went on to the next customer. He would tip his hat back, put on a wide grin and burst into an enthusiastic Italian song. The clanging bell accompanying him told every housewife that the tinker man was here again. ❖

Getting Around Town

Chapter Four

There was a time when women and automobiles just didn't go together. I don't say that to demean them; it was just one of the facts of life back in the Good Old Days. Getting around town was usually something that was handled by the menfolk.

My Grandma Tate never drove, and neither did Grandma Stamps, my mother's mother. Mama herself did get a driver's license, but never drove except when absolute necessity forced her. When Janice married me at the tender age of 18, neither she nor her mother drove. After four years of marriage, she found her way to the driver's seat of our old Ford.

So, I became a driving instructor. After several weeks of coughing starts and burning clutches in big parking lots and along quiet country roads, she had the courage to brave city driving. To be honest, that made *me* more of a nervous wreck than her. Along city sidewalks there were more obstacles for her to maneuver around than out on our farm.

Turns at intersections probably caused more consternation than any other part of the traumatic experience. If Janice turned too sharply, the back wheel would mount the curb and jolt us unceremoniously when we found the pavement again. Compensating for that, she turned too widely and nearly into the path of oncoming cars. And coming to stops took me back to the days of Daddy teaching me to drive: "Kenny," he'd say, "put on the brake. *Brake*. BRAKE!"

If I have high blood pressure today, it was probably rooted in those white-knuckled driving lessons all those decades ago.

She was more intent on wondering how she would look in that brand-new car.

Then a marvelous thing happened. Janice went from being scared to drive in town to actually enjoying it! No more waiting for me to take her shopping, as her mother and grandmothers before her had. She had the freedom to go where and when she wanted.

I remember the first time she chauffeured me, not in a driving lesson, but just because it was a beautiful spring day. She wanted me to go along for the ride. She bought some flowers to set out in her flower bed, and a potted violet to put in the kitchen window. But I think it was just an excuse to let me know I could give my white knuckles a rest.

Finally the day came when I knew it was time to make another magical transition. We graduated from a one- to a two-car family. Visiting the Ford dealership, I ceremoniously kicked the tires and looked under the hood with the salesman while she took it all in. To one degree or another, I'm sure she was more intent on wondering how she would look in that brand-new car.

Since then, she has safely seen countless miles in all of the cars we have purchased, and ultimately, worn out since those early days. She and I now enjoy more leisurely trips. And yes, I let her drive most of the time. It's a way for me to tip my hat to my dear wife.

This chapter looks at all of those wonderful ways of getting around town. From the automobile to the trolley to the elevated train to the interurban, you'll be taken back to the time when just getting there was part of the joy of city life back in the Good Old Days.

—*Ken Tate*

Riding the Trolley With Grandma

By Madeline J. Huss

G randma lived up the street from us. But all she had to do to contact our family was climb the stairs to her second-floor back porch and give a shout. When my mother and her brothers and sisters married, Grandma insisted that they all choose homes within calling distance. Phones weren't common during the Depression of the 1930s, so Grandma selected her own unique method of keeping in touch with her family.

Grandma was not averse to walking the block and a half to our house if there was no answer to her calls. Momma was the one she usually called on, as she lived closest and didn't hesitate to do her bidding, no matter how busy she might be with her own household chores.

> *I complained about it, but secretly, I didn't mind joining Grandma as companion and translator.*

Grandma had immigrated to the United States early in the century. Grandpa had sent money for her to join him in the new country, where he'd found work building the railroad. Not knowing a speck of English, it took all her courage to pack her belongings and make the trip across the high seas with my mother and her sisters and brother.

When she arrived at Ellis Island, she was greeted by Grandpa, who herded the family together and took them to their new home in northern New Jersey. New York City and its environs were too crowded for his liking. Instead, the family moved into a two-story house with a backyard large enough to plant a garden with vegetables and fruit trees. He even had a grape arbor loaded with purple and white grapes.

But Grandma found things difficult in the new country. She could only communicate in Italian with the local butchers and bakers. When she had to go into town to buy a new corset or a spool of black thread, she had to take the trolley.

For some reason, Grandma preferred me among all my cousins to accompany her when she needed to take a trolley trip to the main shopping center in the next town. Besides the five-and-ten, there were several stores there where she could buy dry goods and sewing supplies. At 12, I was the right age to accompany her. I complained to Mama about having to go with Grandma, but secretly, I didn't mind joining her as companion and translator. It made me feel important that she trusted me to act as her guide. We held hands as we boarded the steps of the trolley after it had clanged to a stop. We chose seats on the shady side of the vehicle.

I loved shopping from store to store. The five-and-ten was, of course, my favorite. And I admit, I didn't like the corset store—all those contraptions to squeeze one's body! As I fretted, Grandma took her time and tried on nearly every corset in the store. When she finally made up her mind, and we were walking out of the store, she said, "When you get big, I buy you one too."

Thanks, but no thanks, Grandma, I thought, not daring to express my thoughts aloud. Grandma wasn't one of those smiling grandmas. She always wore a stern expression, and when she told me to do something, I didn't dare refuse.

On icy mornings I went with her to Sacred Heart Church to attend Mass and help her climb the church steps. Of course, she always chose the 6:30 a.m. Mass, so I had to jump out of bed in the dark. My teeth chattered as I ran to Grandma's house to meet her.

I was a teenager when Grandpa died, and after that, Grandma called on me more often. She came to depend on me just at the time when

I began to want to spend more time with friends my own age.

Grandma was persuaded to join a group of older residents—now we'd call them "senior citizens"—to take bus trips to various points of interest. I called the group "Grandma's ladies." Most were widows who didn't know what to do with themselves after their husbands had passed away, and their children were grown and out on their own. She asked me to go with her on most of the trips. New York City was

Pictured here (left to right) are John, Paul, Grandma, Rocco, Grandpa, Mary, Rose (the author's mother) and Sylvia.

close by, and I had the opportunity to go to the Statue of Liberty. We even toured the entire city on a double-decker bus.

Then Grandma and I began to go to the movies together. She didn't understand the plot or what the characters were saying, so I spent most of the walk home explaining the movie we had just seen. She disagreed with my views, however, and enjoyed the show in her own way.

I helped her study for her citizenship papers, and when she passed with flying colors, no one could have been happier than I was.

These days, many grandparents live far from their families. They move to retirement communities or gad about on their own in huge motor homes. At the time, I might have resented all the time I had to spend as Grandma's companion. But now, memories of those times fill a space in my heart, and I am grateful that I had the opportunity to accompany Grandma on her travels. ❖

A Golden Opening

By Carolyn Lathrope

I lived in an exciting city when I was a child. Our family moved to San Francisco in 1934, when I was 7 years old. I was the oldest of four children, with three younger brothers. We lived in an area of the Mission District known as Eureka Valley. I attended Alvarado School just a block from our home. I roamed the city during daylight hours with a city map that my daddy had given me.

Our nearest playgrounds were Douglass and Dolores parks. It was a big adventure to go to the amusement park known as Playland at the Beach. Tickets for kids were 5 cents. Carfare was also a nickel. Movies were a dime.

We lived at 21st and Douglass. Our closest movie houses were the Palmer, on 24th Street, and the Castro, near 17th Street. In 1936, the Noe was built at 24th and Noe. The first feature at the new Noe starred Clark Gable in *Cain and Abel*, with Marion Davies. Of course, I was there! The Palmer closed soon thereafter.

In 1936, my daddy started working for the U.S. Customs Service and began getting a one-month vacation every year. We loved Yosemite National Park. Sometimes chunks of ice from the Sierra Nevada Mountains floated in the Merced River, but we went swimming anyway.

Once, on a ferry ride to Sausalito, we noticed construction going on right in the bay. Daddy said that by May 1937, a giant bridge would be built over the bay. He promised us that he would take us to walk over the bridge on the opening day. In early May there was a fiesta that lasted for a week. We wore Mexican costumes and hats. Excitement over the new bridge was at a fever pitch.

In school, we learned how the big cable was spun from thousands of pencil-sized steel cables bound together with more steel. We were also told that the new structure would be the longest single-span bridge in the world.

Finally the big day arrived—May 27, 1937. We awoke at 3 a.m., packed a big lunch of bologna sandwiches, cookies and apples, and walked down to Market Street to take the streetcar.

We transferred to the cable car at Powell Street. By 5:30 a.m. we were approaching the bridge. It was foggy and cold, but it was beautiful.

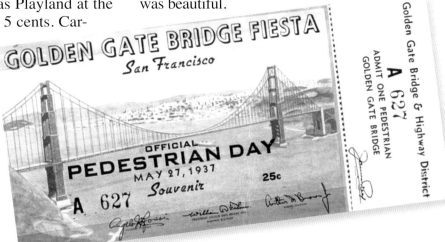

A souvenir pass for walking across the Golden Gate Bridge in San Francisco on Pedestrian Day, May 27, 1937.

It cost a nickel each to walk across. We looked way down to the water. We ran back and forth across the bridge, first looking out to the Pacific Ocean and then back to San Francisco Bay.

Finally, when we got to the north tower and the Marin County Line sign, Daddy took a picture of my three brothers—Bud, who was almost 9; Jim, 7; and Charlie, 5—and me with his Brownie box camera. Charlie fell asleep on the streetcar on the way home, but Daddy said that he was the best hiker.

Fifty years later, in May 1987, some of us crossed the bridge again. This time the bridge was crossed by an estimated 800,000 people. ❖

The Bridge

By Dorothy Stanaitis

We were Philadelphians—always had been. We loved the beautiful brick row homes, majestic cathedrals and splendid neighborhood churches of our city. The vibrant local shopping areas throbbed with energy, while the grand department stores of the central city offered dazzling arrays of elegant merchandise of all sorts.

Philadelphia cultural life was outstanding. It ran from the country's first zoological garden to multiple museums, theaters, concert halls, libraries and many other opportunities for educational amusement. And of course, there were the parades.

Every holiday, special event or change of season brought another fabulous display of marching bands, floats and fun. The Mummer's Parade, held on New Year's Day, was a pageant of feathers and sequins. The local Benevolent Order of Elks' parades radiated patriotism.

But our hands-down favorite was the annual Thanksgiving Day parade. It was our opportunity to get a helium balloon to hold, a soft pretzel to eat, and the chance to give our Santa Claus letters to the volunteer mailmen who marched the parade route, wheeling their mail carts.

We loved the fantastic floats, costumed characters and the excitement of watching Santa arrive and climb several stories of a fire-truck ladder to enter Toyland at Gimbels Department Store, where he would set up his workshop and receive visitors until Christmas.

After Christmas, we would enjoy sledding on George's Hill and ice-skating on Concourse Lake in Philadelphia's magnificent Fairmount Park. There, we could also visit historic monuments, mansions and buildings, including Horticultural Hall, which had been part of the Sesquicentennial Celebration.

We especially looked forward to the day when the banana trees growing inside the hall would bear fruit that the guards would pick and give to any children lucky enough to be visiting.

Pennsylvania and New Jersey meet at the center of the Walt Whitman Bridge. The author is pictured on the left with the stroller at the grand opening of the bridge.

In the spring, we enjoyed Smith Memorial, the Civil War monument that we called "the whispering bench." If you sat on one end of the semicircular marble bench, leaned your head against the back of it and whispered, the person sitting far away at the other end could hear every word clearly. We sent many secret messages back and forth there.

It was also a treat to visit the Japanese pagoda and garden located near the huge fountain of Moses holding the Ten Commandments tablets.

During the hot city summers, Fairmount Park offered shady picnic groves near lakes, ballfields, fields of clover and daisies for making chains, and the fun of rolling down George's Hill until we were giddy with dizziness.

The city arranged for free outdoor movies to be shown in the park at night. Families brought their blankets and pillows and picnic suppers.

We loved the park, and we loved Philadelphia—but something was missing.

Our mother had been a country girl, and her love had been to roam the fields, woods and orchards surrounding her childhood home. She planted a beautiful flower garden in our postage-stamp–size Philadelphia backyard.

But as nice as it was, it wasn't enough. She wanted her children to be able to wade and fish in streams that didn't require an hour's bus ride to reach. She wanted her children to roam barefoot daily in meadows and orchards, not wait for a special trip to the park. She wanted for them what she had enjoyed as a child.

So it was decided. We would move across the Delaware River from Philadelphia into rural New Jersey, the Garden State. It took a long, painstaking search to find just the right house in just the right spot, but Mother did. Sad to be leaving our wonderful city, but excited to be going to the country, we moved away.

We thought our new home was just perfect—a cozy bungalow situated among fields and surrounded by many large trees, just right for hanging swings and building tree houses. We walked up a dirt road to our new school. Mother planted several beautiful flower gardens and a large vegetable patch, which yielded many good things to enjoy in season and to preserve for winter.

We fished and waded in nearby streams, gathered wild berries for pies and picked fruit from local orchards. We were happy—but we never forgot our old home back in the city. Our hearts were in both places, and we loved each for its own special opportunities.

So we grew up in the country and visited the city whenever we could manage it. We went back to visit our old friends and to go to the zoo, the museums and the theater. And we always went to the Thanksgiving Day parade. But those

We heard something very exciting: A new bridge was to be built, linking New Jersey to Philadelphia.

trips were big projects, demanding a great deal of time and money as we negotiated buses, the Speedline, elevated trains and trolleys.

Then we heard something very exciting: A new bridge was to be built, linking New Jersey to Philadelphia. There were other bridges doing the same thing, of course, but none were convenient for us. The new Walt Whitman Bridge would be perfect for tying together our two special places.

We watched every step of construction, groaned at every delay and waited, endlessly it seemed, until the project was complete and the bridge opening was announced. At last we could quickly and easily go back and forth between the states.

On beautiful, sunny May 15, 1957, people were invited to walk across the bridge before it was opened to traffic. We were among the first to rush onto the span. We hurried to the center of the bridge where a dividing line had been painted and marked with "PA" on one side and "NJ" on the other. It was a special day, and it marked the first of many easy, quick trips over the Delaware River.

Even today, on each of those trips, I love to see the Philadelphia skyline as we approach it, just as I love seeing the view into New Jersey on our return. But the best part is always when we reach the peak of the bridge, the spot where New Jersey and Philadelphia, my two favorite places, meet. ❖

The Interurban

By Perry E. Piper

The last official run of an Interurban car in Illinois was in April 1956 when some 2,000 devotees and railroad "nuts" filled three cars for a last trip from Springfield to St. Louis. The advent of good roads and affordable automobiles had eroded the Interurbans' half-century hold on the traveling public's purse.

The trolleylike cars first appeared in 1880; at their peak of popularity, they traveled more than 18,000 miles of track—1,422 miles on them in Illinois. Much of the Illinois mileage served the sprawling suburbs of St. Louis and Chicago, where the North and South Shore lines carried Wisconsin and Indiana commuters to the Chicago Loop.

I often rode the line when I was working out of North Chicago in the late 1960s. As I recall, the fare was a very reasonable 70 cents for the 40-odd-mile ride into the Loop. The cars stopped right in front of the YMCA Hotel, where I had a clean, respectable room that cost $2, with a bath just a step down the hall.

In spite of their frequent stops, the cars ran on a very tight schedule.

In downstate Illinois, the Illinois Traction Co. survived long after many of the other lines had quit. This rail line ran from Ridge Farm up through Danville and over to Champaign and Decatur, and then north through Clinton to Bloomington, and on to the Mackinaw Junction, where it merged with the Peoria cars to head for Springfield and St. Louis.

The Pullman Car Co. in Bloomington built the cars with berths 6 inches longer than those for the railroads and equipped each with a plush-lined "safety" box. Attending porters served juice and rolls in the morning and shined the patrons' shoes overnight. But modernized roads and high-speed automobiles ended this phase of service.

Although freight provided the revenue needed to keep the Tractions running, their primary interest was always in their passengers, and the riders liked it that way. The motorman/conductor, who was sometimes the only employee on board, was most obliging. The cars would stop at most any crossroad to take on or unload passengers or freight, and the employees would even assist heavily laden travelers on and off the cars. How about that? "The Traction," as it was usually called, had clean, elaborate stations in the center of towns such as Bloomington, Decatur and Champaign, and they were open 24 hours a day.

This dedication to service and the low fares allowed ordinary folks to ride the Traction. It is said that the cartoon feature *Toonerville Trolley* was patterned after the Interurban.

Farmers often flagged down the cars and loaded on baskets of eggs, cans of cream and crates of chickens, and the cars obligingly stopped near the marketplace in town. Because of this frequent scheduling and convenient service, shoppers found the Traction an ideal way to spend a few hours in Terre Haute, Decatur or Peoria and still be home at milking time.

I first became familiar with the Traction in 1930, when I registered at the University of Illinois. With the country in the grasp of the Depression, many of my classmates found they could live at home and use the Traction's convenient schedules to commute from Decatur and Danville to classes at the university.

"The terminal," as it was usually called, was powered by an overhead electric line. The cars could attain speeds of 80 miles per hour, and often did. In spite of their frequent stops for passengers and freight, the cars ran on a very tight schedule. Their average speed was about 30–35 miles an hour — not bad when one remembers that in 1928, Illinois had just set a new statewide speed limit of 35 miles per hour.

Many seats on the car were woven cane. Over the years, it broke down and held tight the dirt and insects that were constantly picked up by the coaches as they rumbled along past plowed fields, mosquito bogs and grain elevators with the windows wide open in the summer.

The cars could be controlled from either end, so there was no need to turn the car. A long contact pole on top of the car made connection with an overhead electric wire to give power to the motor. When the car was to be reversed, the pole pointing north was pulled down and locked in place and the south-pointing pole was raised to make contact with the power.

As on streetcars, the seat backs were reversible, so long-distance riders could face forward, backward or both. Passengers often enjoyed four-handed card games as they traveled.

The line that ran from downtown Terre Haute up through Sandford and Vermilion into Paris was a thriving enterprise for years. Both Brazil and Sullivan were served by short lines running out from Terre Haute. A proposed line to Charleston and Mattoon was never finalized, although a short-lived line did connect Mattoon and Charleston for a time.

During the war years, my dear wife's family lived near St. Louis, and we lived in Bloomington. We often loaded the two kids onto the Traction that ran within a block of our house and traveled to visit Uncle George and the boys. We had to make connections with the Peoria car at the Mackinaw Junction. It took all day, but it was a safe and economical way to travel.

How times have changed is evident from a promotional booklet of those long-ago days:

"With hourly service over the Traction Line to and from Paris and Terre Haute, and good connection over the Big Four, Vermilion is fortunate in transportation facilities.

The station at Vermilion, Ill. Photo courtesy the author.

"As one of the outing points for Paris and Terre Haute, it's also noticeable that what a seashore excursion means to an Easterner on the Atlantic, these delightful urban places will come to mean to dozens of the cities of the Midwest.

"A trip over the Interurban gives one physical and mental refreshment. Besides the enjoyment the trolleys furnish in these outings, the trade and traffic, encouraged by the frequency of the service and their efficiency and convenience, have made them indispensable to the life and progress of every ambitious community.

"They open up better knowledge of 'What's what' in every section they enter. This band of steel welds these great states of Illinois and Indiana together in mutual interest, commercial and social, through this Interurban system of cheap and convenient service."

Wow! How times have changed — and not always for the better. ❖

When Mom Rode the Interurban

By Daryle G. Murray

*I*t was the autumn of 1942. There was a slight bite in the winds in Oklahoma City as a young working woman made her way to the First National Bank Building. She felt thankful for the job she had as an elevator operator in the hub of the city's business district. Her position enabled her to rub elbows with the leaders of the business world, and even the governor on occasion.

During the day, she would pretend that she was an important cog in the corporate wheel, but when her shift was over, she faced the reality of life's struggles as she tried to loosen the grip the Great Depression had placed on her and so many other Oklahomans.

Friday's busy business pace had ended, and now the working girl had the weekend to herself. There was little room in her budget for entertainment, so she decided to walk a few blocks over to Grand and Broadway to the Interurban Trolley Station. The crowd at the station was a mixed lot, with businessmen, families and couples cuddling to keep warm as they boarded the Interurban trolley heading south to Norman.

> *"Families would ride the trolley on the weekends and go to Belle Isle for picnics and outings."*

Norman was the southern route for the Interurban. It pulled out of the station and began to leave the downtown area, heading to the residential areas just a few blocks away. Several soldiers in uniform were on the trolley. The Interurban offered an inexpensive way of getting from the military bases into town to catch a movie or just get away from the base for a while.

The young woman was going to Norman to catch a movie and do a little window-shopping. This was nice entertainment for the evening when you had to make your wartime dollars stretch. She could have taken the bus, but riding the diesel-powered buses just didn't have the same feel as the trolley. Besides, the trolley was powered by electricity and didn't belch out large, black clouds of smoke as it made its way down the steel tracks. Riding on one of the bright red-and-yellow–painted trolleys seemed more like an event than just a means of transportation.

"There was just a feeling of it all being a very pleasant excursion," said my mother as she explained what life was like in those early days of World War II. "The people of Oklahoma City had suffered through the Depression, and although they felt it terrible that the United States had been forced to enter the war, they were willing to sacrifice on the home front for the servicemen who were going off to war. Several things were rationed, and not everyone had cars in those days. The cars that were around," she explained, "were getting pretty old, since no one could buy a new car while the war was going on.

"I used to really enjoy the trolley," she said. "I remember there was a nice amusement park called Belle Isle Park. It was located just east of where the Penn Square Mall now stands. It had a large pavilion and a lake where you could swim and rent rowboats. Families would ride the trolley on the weekends and go to Belle Isle for picnics and outings. It was really a nice place.

"The only thing that remains now is the old, abandoned electrical-generating plant. That old plant used to power the trolley system in the city. I read that back even before Oklahoma became a state, the real-estate developers were planning a way of selling cheaper properties away from the downtown district. There was a need for transportation to and from work, so this led the developers to organize the early trolley system in Oklahoma City.

"I was reading an article just the other day that said the city wants to bring the trolleys back to Oklahoma City. Since they have developed the old warehouse district downtown and turned it into a restaurant and entertainment area, and now that they have built the new Bricktown Ballpark, they want to run a trolley system from out near the Will Rogers Airport all the way into downtown for the Bricktown business district."

There was a sparkle in her eyes as she talked excitedly about bringing back a part of her past. "You know, the old trolley system just sort of faded away after the end of the war. The GIs returned home, and those who could bought new cars, and soon the building boom started, and people moved to the suburbs, away from the downtown area. The last run of the trolley was in September of 1947. That was just a month before you were born," she said. "You missed out on all the fun!" she added, a bit of sadness in her voice.

"Oh well, sounds like you may be able to enjoy the new trolleys when they come. I bet it won't be too long because they're looking for

These interurban cars were on their way from the manufacturing plant to Ames, Iowa. Note that the electrical components are missing from the top of the cars.

ways to cut down on pollution, and maybe that would be a way of people getting around without everybody having to drive cars to get where they are going."

It seems a bit odd that an idea that many people thought had vanished forever has now resurfaced. When city elders found the idea once again and dusted it off, it didn't seem so antiquated. Modern talk of electric-powered, nonpolluting transportation seems to blend with the old way of doing things. Maybe in the not-too-distant future, a young working woman will find herself on a crisp fall evening boarding the new Interurban for an outing to a nearby city, perhaps to catch a movie or do some window-shopping. ❖

The World of Tomorrow

By Eileen Higgins Driscoll

I was 13 in 1939 when our seventh-grade teacher, Miss Ellingham, took our class from P.S. 222 to the World's Fair. We lived in Brooklyn, N.Y., and the fair was a bus ride and a subway ride away, in Queens. The fair was a celebration of the 150th anniversary of George Washington's inauguration as first President of the United States.

We were all very excited about our day trip; we didn't get to go to many shows during the Depression. I think it cost us each a quarter for admission. It was probably one of the most memorable days of my elementary school years.

The fair was advertised as "The World of Tomorrow." It certainly did give us a peek at things we would see in the future. "Trylon" and "Perisphere" were new words to us; they were objects that became the official logo for the fair. The Trylon was a tall, narrow, pointed building many stories tall. The Perisphere was a fat, round, beige ball, half the height of the Trylon, and they were placed next to each other. Homes of the future were shown in the Perisphere.

> *The National Broadcasting Co. showed some surprising technology. They called it "television."*

The National Broadcasting Co. (NBC) showed some of the most surprising technology of the future. They called it "television." Until then, very few people had seen or even known anything about it. But NBC offered a fun and interesting demonstration. We could walk across a stage and see ourselves on a screen on the other side of the room. We waved at ourselves and danced and jumped and laughed at our silly actions. Many people, including me, went around and around in amazement.

NBC had broadcast President Roosevelt at the opening of the fair, making him the first president to be recorded on national television. Of course, it took a long time before color television came into our lives.

If memory serves me correctly, National Cash Register (NCR) surprised everyone with a building designed to look like a cash register. I believe it was NCR that demonstrated computers for the first time. The big machines added numbers faster than we could think. They were presented as something to come in the future. How right they were! However, I doubt that back then they ever thought computers

Facing page: *World's Fair or Bust* by John E. Sheridan © 1939 SEPS: Licensed by Curtis Publishing

would develop into all the technologies we have today. Computers still manage to amaze me.

The showman Billy Rose had the entertaining Aquacade. Every day, the beautiful Olympic star Esther Williams and her friends dove and danced to wonderful music in his pool.

Poster advertising the 1939 New York World's Fair.

I think it was the first time most people ever saw acrobatic tricks performed in the water like that in a live show. The ladies' grace and coordination as they swam and dove into the water from overhead swings was fascinating. In the final act, the ladies formed a flower in the water, and Esther Williams dove from a platform into the flower's center.

Dr. Scholl's had an exhibit too. If you were lucky, you could find an empty chair in their building and rest your tired feet on a massage machine that made you feel good all over. We all waited our turn to try out the massage machines.

General Motors showed us cars of the future. They would reach speeds forbidden back then. Their sleek lines made us all smile. The new designs, with all the chrome and bright colors, were a decided break from the square black cars of the day. I wonder if they had thought about power steering, air-conditioning, CDs and TV in cars at that time.

The health exhibits promised us longer lives than our ancestors'. They have kept their promise. We are living longer and better than ever before.

The fair also had rides that thrilled us on hills and curves, and made us scream in fright and laughter at the same time. The best ride was the Parachute Jump. About six seats for two people each were attached to cables that rose about three stories high. As we ascended slowly, we could see forever across the landscape of buildings. When I looked down, I felt dizzy. But when we hit the top, it clicked, and we floated down slowly. That's when it felt like we had left our stomachs up in the air. Oh, how we yelled! I would love to do it all again!

We managed many food and drink stops along our way through the fair. We drank lots of cream soda and root beer to go with the hot dogs and sauerkraut with mustard. And the ice cream tasted so good in the warm sunshine of that beautiful day!

When dusk finally fell, bright-colored lights came on all around us and made the fairgrounds look like a fairyland.

Miss Ellingham brought home a happy, tired group of boys and girls that evening. I doubt she thought someone would remember her 70 years later. She was a lovely lady. ❖

Third Avenue El

By Gregory J. Christiano

Memories are funny things. Certain ones always stick out in our minds as something unique and special. One experience in particular was riding the elevated trains. Growing up in the Bronx in the 1950s was marvelous for me. My neighborhood was centrally located in the borough, in the Tremont section. This area was serviced by the Bronx extension of the Third Avenue el, and it provided the main means of transportation to the residents there.

In its heyday, the line ran all the way from South Ferry in Manhattan to Gun Hill Road in the Bronx. By 1956, the section below 149th Street had been demolished. The remaining portion became the No. 8 shuttle, running vintage, five-car Low-V–type trains from 149th Street (with a free transfer to the IRT) up to Gun Hill Road, where it connected to the White Plains Road Line.

I was always fascinated by the elevated railway. I had even constructed a scale model using my Erector Set and Tinker Toys, running my Lionel trains over a propped-up version of the line! With an imaginary third rail, I'd operate those trains like a regular engineer, stopping at stations to pick up passengers.

The el was part of my neighborhood. It was like arteries pumping the lifeblood of people on the move.

I marveled at the real el's construction. I often wondered how a massive, five-car train that weighed tons could be supported by such an insubstantial-looking structure. It appeared to be a skeleton laid bare, resting upon rows of thin girders. *It must be a deception of engineering know-how*, I thought.

The stations were Victorian-style masterpieces of design. Built mostly of wood with ornamental wrought-iron trim and steel supports, they had stained glass windows and doors. There was always a potbellied stove in the center of the station, on top of planks of hardwood flooring.

In 1953, for the first time, tokens were introduced by the Transit Authority. After purchasing your token at the token booth for 15 cents, you'd drop it through a slot in a huge wooden turnstile. This was another artfully designed piece of Gothic workmanship. In fact, everything about the el—from its station design and catwalks to its entrances and construction—was from a bygone era, a living monument to nostalgia.

As a young boy, I took many trips on the elevated. I entered the 183rd Street station, just a short walk from my apartment building on 184th Street and Washington Avenue. I accompanied my parents on those occasions. But one day in 1956, I decided to venture out on my own. I was 9 years old.

I had no particular destination, but I paid my fare, waited for the downtown train and headed right to the front car. Taking a position directly outside the motorman's cabin, I stared intently out the front-door window as the train made its way down the tracks. As the five-car train pulled slowly out of the station, I could hear the pop and sizzle of the connection with the third rail.

Then, off we went, gaining speed, the cars swaying back and forth like a cradle. By the 1960s, they would install governors on the aging trains to regulate their speed at "safe" levels. On this day, however, I felt freedom and excitement as we zipped along over the streets. I was transfixed, intently absorbing all the sights and sounds along the route. The stone-and-brick canyons echoed the noise of the onrushing train. The elevated structure ran above the street at the level of the second and sometimes the third story of the adjacent buildings. I could see into people's living rooms, kitchens, parlors. Occasionally I saw someone leaning out a window, watching the trains go by. I formed a sort of bond with them, a fleeting moment of shared intimacy as we sometimes exchanged glances.

The other passengers in the car ignored each other and me too. Some had their faces buried in newspapers; some read books or magazines; others stared aimlessly out the windows. When I reached 149th Street, the last stop downtown, I simply moved to the last car and took the trip back uptown, continuing my adventure.

The stations at Tremont Avenue and Fordham Road (190th Street) once had been express stops, with double wooden platforms. These platforms were exposed, with no railings. When I was 9 years old, it seemed to me that a sudden gust of wind or one false step would send a person dashing onto the tracks!

Continuing uptown, we passed through the spine of the borough: Mott Haven, The Hub, Melrose, Morrisania, Claremont Village, Crotona Park, Bathgate, Mount Hope, East Tremont, Tremont (my neck of the woods), Belmont, Fordham, Bedford Park, Norwood and finally Williamsbridge. There was St. Barnabas Hospital, with its stately stone building and sumptuous gardens astride the 183rd Street station. Arthur Avenue was nearby in the Belmont section.

Further on, Fordham University at 190th Street was on the right; the Sears Roebuck Tower, with a huge clock, was on the left. Curving up Webster Avenue, we continued north past the Botanical Gardens, and at 204th Street, French Charlie's Field to the right. The trip ended after we turned at a right angle over the Bronx River Parkway to the terminus at Gun Hill Road, making the connection to the White Plains Road Line, and the No. 5 and No. 2 trains.

The train then made its return run downtown again. I got off at my stop at 183rd Street and walked home. I even picked up the *World, Telegram* and *Sun* for my dad at the newsstand under the station stairs.

My parents had had no idea of my

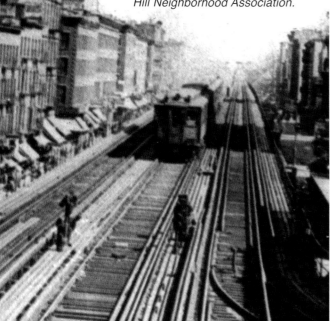

This photo of the Third Avenue el in the Murray Hill area of New York City was taken in 1936. The photo was taken from 34th Street looking north up Third Avenue. Image courtesy of the Murray Hill Neighborhood Association.

whereabouts, or what I had been up to. My father worked the night shift at Bond Bread and slept during the day. My mother worked at Joe Vin Blouse Co. on 187th Street in Belmont. When she got home at around 4 p.m. that day and didn't find me in the apartment, she naturally woke my father. He thought I was playing in the street, as I usually did after school.

I must have timed it perfectly, because it was just about this time that I walked through the front door and saved the local police from a wild-goose chase! I got more than just a bawling out from my parents, but it still didn't deter me from riding my beloved trains. I enjoyed many more escapades, alone and with friends.

Why all the fuss over what many people considered a rickety, noisy, grimy eyesore? To my mind, it was part of our heritage, our history. The el was a national treasure, a magnificent feat of engineering and design. The el was part of my neighborhood. It was like arteries pumping the lifeblood of people on the move. Even with its rattles and screeches, the elevated had special charm, from its gingerbread-style stations to its stained glass windows and quaint, Victorian-style waiting rooms.

The skeletal structure cast its mysterious shadows, a crisscross spiderweb pattern, onto the cobblestone street below. It was mysterious indeed—dark and menacing! And the structure was complemented by the buildings and parks along the route, many of which were distinctive in their appearance. Many were apartment houses with brick, granite and stone facades.

Below were store signs, courtyard entrances and stoops. Above were water tanks and array upon array of TV antennas. Clotheslines filled with laundry hung in the alleyways and on the rooftops. At street level, the familiar bishop's-crook lampposts lined the sidewalks.

Think of a detective yarn or a dark, brooding plot from *film noir* and the stage is set. It's a street scene with a character and personality all its own—a Bronx scene. Now it's gone, lost to us through the cruel fates of time, but preserved in memory—my memory, at least. The rest is for posterity, kept on film, in paintings, prints, photographs and books. The el, once a symbol of progress, has passed into history. ❖

Bus Ride

By Jerry Alston

I turned 8 years old on that hot summer afternoon—July 21, 1945. I was riding on the Seventh Avenue bus with my mom. It was my birthday, and Mom had brought me to Troy as a birthday treat. We had visited several toy stores in search of a present. We found a toy gun at Grant's that I thought was real neat. It was made of metal, which was quite rare because the war had caused a shortage of metal items, especially toys.

Before selecting the gun, we had shopped for some clothes at Wells and Coverly on Fourth Street. Shopping for clothes was not my favorite thing, but knowing I would soon be shopping for my present made it tolerable.

There was an additional bonus to shopping at Wells and Coverly. They had a custom of giving young customers a pie of their choice on their birthday.

I'm not sure how large the selection was because I always opted for my favorite, lemon meringue; it would be dessert for my birthday dinner of roasted leg of lamb, mashed potatoes and green beans. (Even though my birthday usually came on one of the hottest days of the year, and we lived in an upstairs flat without air-conditioning, my mother always prepared her birthday boy's favorite dinner.)

All the seats were filled on the Seventh Avenue bus that hot summer day. The Seventh Avenue was one of three buses that serviced Watervliet then. It was quite common to ride the bus for shopping, going to the movies, football games, school and so forth. Everybody rode the bus to and from the cities and villages in the Albany area.

At the stop at River and Broadway, a rather large black woman got on carrying several shopping bags. As she moved down the aisle, I could tell the heat and her heavy burden were causing her some discomfort.

She glanced at a young man in a suit and tie, and waited for him to remove his outstretched leg from the aisle so she could pass. As she walked toward us, I got up and motioned for her to take my seat. I was always taught to give my seat to my elders and to ladies, and this weary passenger met both qualifications.

It was quite common to ride the bus for shopping, going to the movies, football games, school and so forth.

With a tired smile, she thanked me and sat down next to my mom, saying something in a low voice. My mom smiled. The young man glanced back at us and seemed to fidget in his seat. Mom later said she thought the young man was embarrassed that he hadn't offered his seat. She told me how proud she was when I did. I was confused.

I failed to see any significance in the fact that the woman was black. I was young and had not witnessed bigotry. I lived in a small, parochial world where there was little occasion for such incidences.

Although I failed to appreciate the significance of the event, I still felt good that my mother was so proud of me on that hot summer day more than 50 years ago. Mom has been dead almost 20 years now, and I still miss her. I also miss riding the Seventh Avenue bus. ❖

Dreams of Trains

By Robert Longfield

As a child, I lived in Fargo, N.D. The Southern Pacific Railroad depot was located in the heart of downtown, and the tracks bisected several streets of the city. Each evening at about 8:30, the West Coast Limited came charging into town, and street-crossing gates came down with a flashing of lights and ringing of bells. When the train stopped at the depot, the main street, Broadway, was closed, bringing both auto and foot traffic to a standstill.

With my parents, I was frequently among those obliged to wait for the crossing to be cleared. I remember how exciting it was, watching the big engine huffing and puffing like an exhausted runner, catching its breath.

As it came to a halt, the engineer dropped down from his cab, and with oilcan and flashlight in hand, strolled around his big steed, looking for possible trouble.

As its headlight pierced the darkness ahead, and its bell clanged a warning to dallying passengers to hurry aboard, it seemed impatient to get going.

On cold winter nights, steam exuded from the hoses connecting the cars, and I longed to be one of the people who sat, warm and comfortable, at tables in the dining car, enjoying their evening meal. In the coaches, people were playing cards, reading books or just talking.

Bringing up the rear of the train were the Pullman cars where, already, people were in their berths, staring out the windows. How I envied those passengers in their warm, comfortable "cocoons" aboard the train while we stood waiting in the cold. I wanted to be on that train more than anything.

Suddenly, with an "All aboard!" shout, a *toot-toot* and a hissing of steam, the train slowly moved down the track. The street gates lifted, and the red lights on the rear car disappeared in the distance as it sped on its way to the West Coast.

Several years later, I had the good fortune to be a warm and comfortable kid staring out the window of that train as we stopped at the old familiar depot to board passengers. It was as wonderful as I had anticipated years earlier.

As a teenager in the mid-1930s, I lived on the St. Croix River at Hudson, Wis. Each evening, shortly after 9 o'clock, we would hear the distant whistle of the Elite 400 on its run from Chicago to St. Paul and would watch across the mile-wide river as the streamliner slowly crept up the steep bank on the opposite shore.

With its headlight flashing from side to side and lights glowing from all the windows, it looked like a giant, luminescent worm crawling up the hillside. I never missed watching this nocturnal monster when I was at home, and I always thought how much fun it would be to be a passenger on that wonderful train.

Several years later, another dream came true when, upon returning from Chicago, I was a passenger on the 400. As we approached Hudson, I became more and more excited, wondering if I would be able to see my home across the river. Then, suddenly, there it was, a distant blur of light shining from our big living-room window. My long-standing dream had come true. ❖

Tricycle Trolleys

By John L. Patton

Growing up in the Cincinnati, Ohio, neighborhood of Fairmount in the early 1950s held many special delights. When I was only 2 or 3, I first noticed the trolley that passed our house many times each day. My father told me that it was the last old-time trolley in town. While I don't recall riding that wooden, open-air beauty, I remember I had some wonderful dreams about that trolley.

But I did more than dream. Along with my friend Billy, whose dad worked for the Cincinnati Traction Co., I played trolley driver. Billy's father gave us his out-of-date transfer pads, and we pedaled our trikes up and down the street as if we commanded the Route 49 Fairmount-Downtown-Zoo trolley.

Billy even had a tricycle bell, which he rang as he picked up his imaginary passengers. How I envied Billy that bell! Although I asked for one, I never did get a bell of my own.

All summer long, we rode our tricycle trolleys endlessly to the amusement of neighbors and passersby. One of our regular stops was Mouck's Bakery, where the nice bakery lady would occasionally give us each a thumbprint cookie. Selected friends and neighbors would be offered a transfer, which was accepted with a smile and a chuckle. Art Brestle, who owned the candy store on the next street over, would pass us on his way home and ask if we were on schedule.

I did my best to stay on good terms with Billy, since without him as a friend, I would lose those nifty transfers. But when he got a transfer holder clip and a movable tear-off bar from his dad, our friendship became one-sided. Now Billy could ride our route with his transfers clamped to his handlebars, while I had to keep mine shoved in my back pocket. With all those real bus-driver accessories, Billy began bossing me around and even tried to make me confine my route to his driveway.

Two weeks after I stopped playing trolley driver with Billy, that last trolley made its final run. While there might have been a newspaper story, there was no fanfare, nor ceremony at the end of the route, which was only a block from my house.

One day, I saw a trolley bus instead of a trolley. While the bus had two poles, like the trolley, which received power from overhead wires, the magic was gone forever.

For years, the old rails for that last old-time trolley lay exposed, giving me false hope that the old trolleys might return. Of course, they never did. In time, I accepted—and even enjoyed—riding the nice, new, shiny trolley buses. And when those were finally retired in favor of diesel buses, I noticed, but I didn't really give it a thought. But when those overhead wires were removed from the Fairmount landscape, I had to swallow a lump in my throat.

The new fleet of orange-and-cream buses might have meant progress for the city. But for me, it marked the end of boyhood dreams, games and innocence. History for me is in many ways the same as nostalgia: holding on to the memories of a slower-paced and often more colorful way of life. ❖

My Yellow Dragon

By Cathy Taylor

Those who remember Judy Garland in the movie *Meet Me in St. Louis* can hardly forget the yellow trolley scene or the lilting song that went with it. The trolley played an important role in my life too. During World War II, we moved from our small town to the Twin Cities so Dad could take a job at a war plant. I cried when I left my friends. Luckily, our new home was located on the Como-Harriet streetcar line. Its tracks brought a bright yellow trolley practically to our doorstep. I imagined it offered an endless parade of adventures just for the taking, and I was eager to explore, yet sort of scared too. It was a big, busy world out there.

I learned that if I changed trolleys at certain points using paper transfers from the motorman, I could go anywhere, be it just a few blocks or 9 miles across town to visit cousins. And just think: The ride cost only a dime one way! And if I bought tokens, the cost was just 7½ cents! As we dropped our fares into the square metal box, the coins jingled happily. The motorman even made change when we needed it.

Streetcars had various nicknames: The Trolley, Old Yellow and Yellow Dragon. Their routes crisscrossed the city in all directions so they were convenient for most people. They ran about every 20 minutes all day long. They operated by electric cable. To change his route, the motorman had to stop, get out and switch the tracks.

Our streetcars were enclosed, not the open-air kind. Still, they were drafty—sometimes cold, sometimes hot—and they bumped and swayed as they sped along. Yet to me, they were a marvel. I'd never seen such freedom to come and go.

The hard varnished seats were yellow and arranged like those on a bus, with a row of double seats on each side. At one end, for 10–15 feet, benches lined the windows; these were called the "peanut rows." This left space for people to stand. These passengers grabbed onto straps hanging from the ceiling or handles on the aisle ends of the seats. Keeping one's balance was tricky as the car rocked and rolled when the motorman was trying to make up time.

A trolley sits in front of the railroad depot in Willoughby, Ohio.

Back then, we didn't have shopping malls—only neighborhood business corners with a drugstore, maybe a barbershop, a small grocery, sometimes a movie theater and a beer tavern. Some corners were bigger than others, but all were usually within a short walking distance for most people.

But my yellow friend took me to the wonderful world of downtown, which meant department stores, dress shops and intriguing lunch places like a gypsy tearoom where we had our fortunes read. This was the working girl's Saturday excursion—meeting for lunch and then shopping. We pretended to be so sophisticated in our best dresses, perky little hats and wrist-length white gloves.

Streetcars in 1930s Milwaukee, Wis.

The streetcars were handy for dates too, because all the first-run movies were downtown. During the war, it was rare that a date of mine had his own car. Usually he brought me home, and we'd wait on my front porch for 20 minutes while the streetcar went to the end of the line to turn around and return. When we saw it coming, he'd run to the corner to catch it. If he missed it, that could be bad, for the trolley ran only once an hour after midnight.

But streetcars weren't just for social use. During my high school years, they were my transportation to and from school. We didn't have free school buses. When the weather was good, I walked the mile and a half to school to save the carfare. I also recall streetcars packed full of screaming, cheering students, hanging out the windows, coming from football games.

Trolleys were often the only way for workers to get to their jobs. Every morning, people on their way to work waited at corners with tin lunch boxes, brown paper bags or briefcases. And when I started working, I, too, rode Old Yellow to and from my job every day.

Once I was riding to work and sitting on the aisle seat next to the peanut row. The motorman was rocking his way along the street when he came to an intersection and forgot to stop to change them. Instead of speeding merrily ahead, the car took a sharp left turn.

I found myself suddenly swished out of my seat and on the floor, sitting upright between the peanut rows. I wasn't hurt, but I was stunned into silence until the humor of the situation dawned on me. Then I laughed with my fellow passengers. I never screamed "I'll sue!" It was just one of those funny things that happen.

I'll never forget the time Dad reluctantly allowed me to drive his precious stick-shift car. I was just learning. I backed out of our driveway into the street, and as I crossed both sets of streetcar tracks, I killed the motor. Then I looked up to see streetcars coming from both directions. My heart pounded and I shook. Both trolleys had to stop and wait while I fumbled to restart the car.

Finally I backed on across the street into another driveway. I heaved a sigh of relief as the streetcars hurtled away. Worst of all, Dad had been watching the whole thing from our front porch. That was the one and only time I drove his car.

Then came the 1950s. Everything had to be bigger and better. History was made when the first all-under-one-roof mall was built. However, it was 15 blocks from the closest streetcar line.

Within two years, the streetcars were replaced by smelly, exhaust-spitting buses. When all the streetcar tracks were ripped up, the last traces of our trolleys were gone.

I'll admit that buses were more comfortable and had no peanut rows. Still, losing the Yellow Dragon was like losing an old friend. Whether for economic reasons or in the name of progress, a big chunk of history disappeared with those streetcars, replaced by nostalgia for those good old trolley days. ❖

East Side, West Side

Chapter Five

Mama was really not the disciplinarian of the family. That was usually left to Daddy. I don't know how many times I broke the rules and had to bear the dreaded words: "Just wait until your father gets home!"

But one day was different. As far as I know, it was the only time I truly scared Mama. And I found out quickly that a frightened mother hen sure knows how to peck her chick. And that day, I really ruffled her feathers.

We were in the nearest small city of any size, Branson, Mo., for our weekly shopping, which included a stop at the grocery store. I was probably around the age of 4 or 5, but I remember the incident as clearly as anything from my youngest days.

Mama had a simple rule for her brood when it came to street crossings: Always stay with her. I remember holding only a coattail or even the hem of her dress as she crossed the street carrying grocery bags, or later, my baby sister Donna.

That Saturday afternoon was rainy, and I was anxious to go home. It seemed that we had stood at the grocery's curb for hours as Mama looked first one way and then the other waiting for a big enough break in the traffic to cross the street with her most precious package: me.

At one point, Mama started to step out, but then felt the break in traffic wasn't big enough. The problem was that her step backward didn't take into account the swift little feet at her side.

Her coat slipped out of my grasp, and I went flying out into the street.

Her coat slipped out of my grasp, and I went flying out into the street. There was a shriek, and then Mama was in traffic with me, grabbing the collar of my coat. She pulled me under her one free arm and then we—more she than I—finished the dash across the street as cars missed us by inches.

When we got to the other side, there was swift retribution in the form of a single, but effective, swat to my *gluteus maximus*. That was a shock! Mama never spanked. She always left that to Daddy. I didn't know what to say or do, so I was simply quiet. Mama was too. Then I saw the streak of a tear and heard a muffled sob.

"I'm sorry, Mama!" I muttered. But even in my childish thoughts I knew that Mama wasn't mad. She was scared.

Future trips to town salved the fright of that day. Mama taught me how to cross streets safely, and I went on to be a newspaper boy with a route that encompassed—as the old song said—"East side, west side, all around the town."

In its own way, that day taught me just how special I was to my mother, knowing that she would literally lay down her life to pull me from almost certain death.

Most of the memories in this chapter are a lot more gentle than mine, but in most the lessons are still the same. They are set in some of those favorite places that we loved to visit back in the Good Old Days. And all of them bring to mind the love and security we could find along the city sidewalks of our youth.

—*Ken Tate*

Ice Cream and Love

By Arthur Jackson

*I*t was a lazy summer evening sometime in the mid-1940s. An east wind blew in from the ocean, carrying the hint of an approaching storm. The birds had settled in their nests, and the neighborhood youngsters had gone home. My mother closed the screen door quietly and joined me on the porch. She patted me on my shoulder. "I have a taste for ice cream," she declared.

I jumped up eagerly. "I'll go get it."

"I have a better idea," she replied. "Why don't we just take a walk together? We can stop at the store on the way home and pick out whatever we want."

"Sounds great." And together we headed down the walk. My mother and I did a lot of walking together. Sometimes we went to the supermarket or to the drugstore. Other times we just strolled through the neighborhood together.

She always seemed to appreciate my company on these outings. "If I walk by myself," she would say, "I have nobody there to talk with."

> *"If I walk by myself," Mother would say, "I have nobody there to talk with."*

Our neighborhood in Jamaica, N.Y., consisted mainly of one- and two-story homes, and for the most part, it was a friendly community. People usually took time to pass the time of day when they met you on the street or if they were outside doing yard work. Almost every yard contained flower beds, and Mother always stopped to chat with fellow gardeners when we passed.

"Hi there, Mrs. Jackson," a lady called as she straightened up and stretched her tired back. Mother was well known for her gardening ability. She seemed to possess the proverbial green thumb. Many sought her help to restore health to their ailing greenery. "How are you this evening?"

"I can feel a lot of dampness in the air," Mother said. "We might get rain before long."

"That's good." The lady sounded more cheerful now. "Rain will be a good thing. Do the flowers good."

Mother stooped to pick up a branch that had fallen across the path.

"Nice talking to you, Mrs. Adams. We best be on our way."

In later years, I have wondered why I was the only one of her children to accompany her on her walks. I had a sister and a brother. They were, however, quite a bit older than I was, so I may have been enjoying a privilege saved for the youngest of her brood.

I learned a lot about my mother on these walks, and this was undoubtedly a good influence on my behavior. Mother was always on the lookout for any way she could improve our surroundings. She spoke encouragingly to neighbors who were making improvements around their homes and yards; she removed sticks and rubble from the sidewalks and set aside toys that had been left carelessly in the path. Wherever she went, she improved things.

Many times I saw her run into the street to retrieve a ball or toy before some child could venture into traffic. At those times she would remark, "I just can't understand why some folks let those little tykes run around any which way. Someone should be responsible for them."

How often I have recalled those words!

Up one block and down another we traveled. It seemed to me that we had gone at least a mile.

"My legs are tired," I protested at last.

"Nonsense." Mother chuckled. "Son, don't you know the more walking you do, the less pains you'll get in your legs? I've told you before, walking is good exercise."

Now we were walking along the avenue, which served as a boundary for our neighborhood. A car passed slowly, then stopped and backed up until it was beside us. "Say, Miss," someone called from the car, "can you tell us the way to Ashberry Avenue?"

Mother paused a moment. Then she pointed. "Ashberry is about 12 blocks down that way."

The driver thanked her and drove on down the street. I started trying to urge her to walk faster because I knew our destination was not far away.

"Well, hello there, Arthur," the owner called as we entered his store. "I don't often see you here in the middle of the week."

"My mother wants ice cream, and she

knows where to find the very best kind," I said slyly. Did I think my praise might gain me a larger scoop of ice-cold bliss?

Mother laughed. "Now look, young man, I can speak for myself. What I want is …"

"Vanilla!" I burst in. "She always wants vanilla. It's all she ever chooses."

"I remember," the owner said, smiling. "And I suppose you want …"

"Strawberry, like always," I announced triumphantly.

Before long, we were on our way home, contentedly enjoying our treat, and waving and nodding to friends who were sitting on their porches, enjoying the cool evening breeze. Mother glanced down at me and pretended to be shocked. "Arthur, take your time," she chided. "You'll have it gone before we get to the corner."

I must have curbed my enthusiasm, because I clearly remember that I had plenty of ice cream left when we reached the corner. We waited there for the traffic to clear the main intersection.

"It's all clear," Mom announced. "Let's go."

As we stepped out, looking forward, we heard a screech of brakes behind us. The car was making a right turn and was headed straight for us.

I grabbed Mother's arm, pushing her sideways. Then I was on the ground with an enormous pain throbbing through my leg. Tires squealed as the car sped away, leaving us there in the intersection. I tried to get up, but I couldn't. I knew something was seriously wrong with my right leg.

In a very short time, I found myself in our local emergency room. Mother was with me. She kept twisting her hands together and asking over and over, "What happened, Arthur? It

went so fast I didn't even see what happened."

I remembered to be brave. "Don't worry, Mother. My leg will be just fine. It's the same one I broke in the park a couple of years ago. Remember?"

Later, the nurse smiled as she handed me my new crutches. "You are a brave boy, Arthur," she said seriously. "If you hadn't moved so fast, your mother would have been struck by that car."

_____ ✦✦✦ _____

Did I think my praise might gain me a larger scoop of ice-cold bliss?

_____ ✦✦✦ _____

I thought about that when we were on our way home in the taxi. What would we ever have done if that car had hit Mother? I couldn't bear to even think about that.

Nevertheless, when I settled back into the cushions, I gave a little groan. "Does your leg hurt, Arthur?" Mother asked sympathetically.

"No, Mother, my leg's all right," I sighed. "But the bad part is that I never did get to finish my ice-cream cone!"

I harbored a secret hope that we might go back for another cone when I could walk again, but that never happened. For the rest of that summer, Mother could not bear to walk that direction again.

Sixty years have passed. My mother has passed on to her eternal reward, but she still lives and walks, tall and strong, in my memory. I see her down on her knees, tending her garden, hanging up the laundry on a fresh, windy spring morning, and clipping fragments from ailing plants as she tries to rescue them.

Someday I would like to go back to our old neighborhood in Jamaica. That ice-cream store may no longer be there; even if it is, all the people I knew are gone. Still, walking those familiar blocks and remembering would be a real delight. Even though I would no longer have my mother there, her memory would walk with me. ✦

Bay Ridge in the 1940s

By Randi Ryan

As a grade-schooler, I was a city kid for most of the year. Back in the 1940s, folks who lived in the Bay Ridge neighborhood of Brooklyn in New York City were much more homebound than people usually are today. We walked everywhere. Moms did their shopping almost every day.

I often accompanied my mom on her shopping rounds. Pushing my baby sister in a carriage, we walked to the nearby business district where there was a grocery, a fruit-and-vegetable man, a butcher, a bakery and a "candy store" where dads bought the morning paper on their way to the subway for their commute to work. Our subway station was on 69th Street in Bay Ridge, just a few blocks from both the Staten Island ferry and our apartment home between 71st and 72nd on Colonial Road.

I knew that shopping run as well as Mom did. I can still picture the greengrocer, with his bristly, black mustache, his cheery way of joking with customers in his rolling Italian accent, and his big white apron that picked up his handprints after he broke the greens off the carrots and beets. Sometimes he gave me a little carrot to munch on—yum! Mom bought those and more—yellow or white turnips, cabbage, a batch of potatoes.

She'd plan it out, of course, so as not to buy everything at once. That would be too heavy a load, and we still had to stop at the butcher. He had helpers and a high glass case and lots of saws and blades for cutting meat on massive butcher blocks. Most of the meat was cut to order, though the noise from the meat grinder made it hard to shout loudly enough so he could hear. He was a burly, smiling, grandfatherly fellow with a white mustache. He didn't talk much to kids.

I stood quietly by Mom, swirling circles in the sawdust on the wooden floor with my feet while he sliced bacon and wrapped stew beef. Everything was wrapped in paper in those days, and shoppers put the parcels in their own bags.

It was time to move on, with a quick stop at the greeting-card store so Mom could return her library book. The pay library gave you a three-day loan for a small fee—a quarter, I think—and Mom, who was an avid reader, usually had books coming and going.

Onward we went to the bakery across the street, our final stop, for whole wheat bread, or rye, and something for a treat with after-dinner coffee.

She spoke Norwegian with the staff while

> *Our bakery was Scandinavian; our neighborhood a broad mix of German, Irish and Nordic.*

choosing a few éclairs, or a seven-layer chocolate cake, or maybe Napoleons, or Danish pastries with apricot filling.

The lady tended to my priorities: "Would you like a cookie, dear?"

Of course I would! "Yes, thank you," I answered politely, and she passed me a small, buttery treat edged with chocolate.

Of course, I murmured my polite thank-you in Norwegian; I was in the habit of switching back and forth in this multilingual, multiethnic corner of the metropolis. Our bakery was Scandinavian; our neighborhood a broad mix of German, Irish and Nordic. My childhood girlfriends covered a varied spectrum, and we hopscotched together in English.

Finally ready to be on our way—tired from all the walking and toting and visiting and shopping—it was time for us to head home for lunch. I hoped for canned tomato soup and grilled cheese, my favorite, and looked forward to tomorrow and our next trip to the shops! ❖

Fabulous Fluoroscope

By Richard Steele

When I came across the picture of a "foot-viewer," as Mom always called it, the photo brought back vivid memories of the first time I saw one, in the mid-1940s.

Mom had taken me downtown one summer afternoon to shop for a new pair of shoes. My two brothers and I got only one pair each year, just before the start of school in the fall. Most mothers bought footwear for their kids at J.C. Penney's, but I had a narrow foot, and it was hard to find shoes that fit properly. The only store that stocked narrow widths was Winslow Shoes, one of the most expensive shops in town.

After getting off the city bus at the downtown stop, Mom and I walked across the street and went into Winslow's.

A shoe-fitting fluoroscope.

There, prominently displayed in the middle of the store, was a "shoe-fitting fluoroscope." I had no idea what it was, or what it did.

The salesman had me step up onto the platform and told me to put my feet inside the machine while the three of us peered through the viewing windows. Mom's broad smile matched mine as we looked down at the glowing bones in my feet! My year-old, worn-out shoes were way too tight, and when the man told me to wiggle my toes, I could barely make them move.

After having me try on a new, larger pair, the salesman told me to stick my feet into the device again. As I happily wiggled my toes in the greenish-yellow glow, he shrewdly pointed out to Mom how the "scientifically fitted" shoes gave my feet room to grow and allowed them to move freely.

The gimmick worked. Mom was sold, and though they cost more than she had hoped to pay, I proudly wore my "special" shoes on the way home to break them in.

Before long, it seemed that every kid who went downtown ran to Winslow's to look at the bones in his feet. An X-ray was something they'd never seen before—and it was free to look! Boys took turns sticking their feet in the machine while their buddies looked down into the device, telling each other to wiggle their glowing, irradiated toes!

The store employees were tolerant at first, figuring it would lure in more adults and increase sales as word about the fluoroscope spread around town. But the almost-constant stream of kids going in and out proved disturbing to Winslow's upscale clientele, and they soon limited use of the machine to their adult customers only, or kids with their parents in tow.

Very little was known then about the dangers of prolonged exposure to radiation; paying customers could linger as long as they liked, looking at their feet bones through the amazing device.

In time, of course, the novelty of the machines wore off. They began disappearing from the stores as concerns grew over the potentially damaging effects of being over-irradiated.

When I think back to those days, I remember how awestruck I was when I looked down at my feet and saw in the ghostly glow how my greenish-yellow toes were joined together. In spite of the risk involved, I wouldn't have wanted to miss that experience for anything. ❖

Mr. Bishop

By Selma McCarthy

*I*n the 1930s there was a quaint little hat-blocking shop on Main Street in my hometown of Vincennes, Ind. It was owned by Mr. Bishop, a kindly little man who loved everyone—especially children. Along one wall of his shop were rows of freshly cleaned and blocked hats waiting to be picked up by their owners.

In those days, most men wore hats, especially when they dressed up. No self-respecting man would go out without one; he might miss the opportunity to tip it to a beautiful woman.

Directly across from the rows of hats were four shoeshine chairs lined up against the wall. The "shoeshine boy" was kept busy cleaning and buffing the gentlemen customers' shoes. This happy, smiling boy put on quite a show with his shine cloth. After applying Shinola Wax Shoe Polish to the shoes, he would whip the cloth across the toes in a rhythmic fashion and even do a little dance step now and then, keeping time with the polishing cloth. His smiling face and dancing feet garnered him extra money in tips over and above the 10 cents paid for the shine. His rhythm and dance steps delighted his customers. The male shop owners on Main Street kept Mr. Bishop and the shoeshine boy busy, helping them maintain their grooming of hats and shoes.

Dress suits, starched white shirts, ties, gleaming, polished shoes and a freshly blocked hat were absolute "musts." The casual look was unheard of except for fishing, hunting or loafing at home.

In the summer, Mr. Bishop placed a popcorn machine outside his shop. The aroma was irresistible and drew kids who had a nickel to spend—and some who didn't, like Darlene and me.

Back then, it was safe for children to go downtown on Saturday to window-shop and wish. My best friend, Darlene Dutton, and I would go every Saturday, and when we had a nickel, we would hurry to Mr. Bishop's shop to buy his scrumptious popcorn. He filled the bags till they nearly overflowed. Bless him! He must have known how poor we were. I'm sure our shabby clothes and scuffed shoes were a tip-off.

One Saturday, the aroma of Mr. Bishop's popcorn drew us to the machine, though we didn't have a copper to our names. We stood watching the machine spitting out hot, golden kernels as we longed for a nickel. A tear slid down Darlene's cheek, and we turned to go.

"Oh, Mr. Bishop, how can we ever thank you for your kindness?"

Suddenly Mr. Bishop appeared with a big smile on his face. "Hello, girls! Would you like some popcorn?" he asked.

"Oh, yes, we would, but we haven't any money today," I said, hoping that my answer implied that we weren't usually penniless.

"Well, you girls are pretty good customers, and I appreciate repeat business," he said, handing each of us a brimming-over sack of the hot, fresh popcorn. "This time it's free because you're two of my best customers."

"Oh, Mr. Bishop, how can we ever thank you for your kindness?" I asked, holding my popcorn against my chest lest I spill any.

Darlene was all choked up, but she said "Thank you, Mr. Bishop" in a hushed voice.

"Just being you is thanks enough, children," Mr. Bishop said as we turned to go, clutching our treasures.

Mr. Bishop's warm heart touched us in a wonderful way. To this day I still remember his kindness to us, two poor children who didn't even have a nickel for popcorn! He is long dead now, as is Darlene. I hope they met in heaven and are together handing out popcorn to little children. ❖

Facing page: *The Popcorn Man* by Jay Killian © House of White Birches nostalgia archives

The Automat

By Ernest Barra

I get a little sad when I remember the wonderful times I had enjoying snacks at the Automat back during my boyhood days in New York City. It was heartwarming to retreat from the cares and trials of my busy days in the big city to sit down and enjoy those delicious little meals that were very inexpensive.

What I enjoyed most was the privacy as I went from row to row down those columns of trays, each little drawer holding a sandwich, a piece of pie, a salad or whatever else I was looking for. It was nice. The food would just sort of slide out on a tray after I deposited a coin. There it was: a freshly baked potato, or a nice slice of apple pie with cream. Then I just poured myself a fresh cup of coffee and sat down to eat.

> *Each little drawer held a sandwich, a piece of pie, a salad or whatever else I was looking for.*

Others went about their business in the same way. Many read a newspaper or magazine while they ate; it was nice and quiet there, almost like home. There was no hurry about eating. Everything was meant to be convenient and comfortable for the customers, and we took all the time we needed.

Enjoying a quick bite at the Automat was relaxing—a refuge from the hectic pace we generally kept up as we went about our business in the big city. With the subways, busy street traffic, lots of noise and people everywhere, I sometimes felt as if I were trapped in a whirlwind of human hustle and bustle in the struggle to make a living.

That desperate feeling was often followed by pangs of hunger, and then the Automat came quickly to mind. In New York, there was always one nearby; the very sight of one was most welcome. It was a nice place to stop in and rest awhile. And one of the best things about it was the low prices. For only a few cents, I could enjoy a quick, refreshing repast. The food, by the way, was excellent, and the courteous cafeteria workers helped customers in any way needed.

It is with a touch of nostalgic melancholy, therefore, that I wonder why this noble institution disappeared. Why did the Automat fade from the Gotham scene? It was so much a part of the big town! The pace in New York was always fast, and the people were always busy; in that hectic atmosphere, the Automat provided a ready answer with tasty and well-prepared food, and good brewed coffee. It was fun to pour myself a cup; I just dropped a nickel in the slot, held my cup under the spigot and out came fresh coffee. Or, if I preferred, I could get a cup of tea or even hot chocolate; whatever I wanted, I could get it. The Automat was always ready to cater to each customer's palate preferences.

There was something else fun about grabbing a quick bite at the Automat, and that was watching the people from the country—the "out-of-towners," especially the kids—having so much fun dropping their coins in the slots and watching the food slide out. They had a hilarious time! Some of them literally jumped with glee. Obviously the whole business of eating from mechanical gadgets was entirely strange and exciting for them. It was nice to see them enjoy their Automat experience with such delight.

But the Automat is no longer with us, and that's too bad. It was a noble institution, so neatly adapted to the busy lives of city folks.

And its low prices were truly in keeping with the fiscal trend of the Good Old Days, back when a cup of delicious coffee cost only a nickel. ❖

CC's Department Store

By Kathy Manney

When I was growing up in the 1940s and 1950s, the place to shop for clothing was the downtown department store with the intricately hand-painted mannequins in the front window.

Besides the well-known chain stores like Montgomery Ward and J.C. Penney's, Vancouver, Wash., was served by an old, locally owned standby, CC's Department Store. CC's was the kind of store that closed on Sundays and was known for their "better" merchandise.

CC's was nearly a museum, even by 1940s–1950s standards. Shabbily genteel and somewhat dowdy, it had creaking bare wooden floors, a wide wooden staircase and high ceilings. But what really made CC's stand apart from other downtown Vancouver stores was how each transaction was completed.

When you made a purchase in CC's, the clerk handling your transaction put the money into a metal container the size of a soup can and sent it, along with a sale voucher, by electronic wire to a second-floor central cashier. The cashier made change and returned the transaction in the same manner to the clerk so that she could close out the sale with your receipt. CC's is the only store I remember that handled their cash-only transactions in this manner.

Grandma was a regular shopper at CC's. She chose the store especially for their selection of matching Cinderella-brand dresses for my younger sister and me. I remember shopping for back-to-school and Easter clothes there too.

At that time, women "dressed" for downtown shopping expeditions, and customers like my grandmother knew the store's clerks by name. This was a time when there was personalized service. Knowing what Grandma liked to buy for us, clerks sometimes held back Cinderella dresses in our sizes until she had a chance to peruse them.

Left: The author and her sister. Right: The author, her sister and grandmother are dressed for downtown shopping.

Besides purchasing dresses for my sister and me, Grandma sometimes would buy a hat for herself. CC's carried a fine line of women's hats. In the Good Old Days, wearing a hat and gloves was one of the ideal hallmarks of femininity.

Standing on a corner of Main Street, CC's was a large part of downtown Vancouver. It was also part of a more courteous era, when everyday shopping was more formal. People dressed up, rode the bus and took their time browsing through the merchandise. If you went into a store, the owners chatted with you and wanted you to spend some time. It was all part of the local flavor of the Good Old Days. ❖

Hamburgers, Hot Dogs and Chicago

By John N. Doll

Hamburgers are still a favorite in the United States—as are hot dogs—and they're still a favorite of mine. But whether it was good old Chicago or perhaps the difference in price, they tasted the best during the 1930s in Chicago. On the North Side, where Sheffield and Wrightwood crossed Lincoln Avenue next to the car barns, there was a little white tile building called the White Castle. That little building was about 15 x 15 feet, and like all the other White Castles in Chicago, the aroma from their product permeated the air for blocks around. There were no tables and chairs, but a bar about 12 inches wide was mounted around the inside. Standing at the bar, you simply picked up your hamburgers and ate—and ate and ate and ate.

Flukeys sold nothing but hot dogs and soda pop. But everything you could imagine was on the dog.

Those little hamburgers were not much more than a bite-full, about 2½ inches square. But the meat was delicious, with optional mustard or ketchup, a slice or two of dill pickles and onions, all sandwiched between a soft-as-cotton bun. They were 5 cents each. It was possible to order only one, but I never did, nor can I remember seeing anyone else order a single White Castle burger.

In these tiny shops, you received your order directly from the hands of the fry cook. I don't remember the exact size of his grill, but he always seemed to be frying about four dozen at a time with the grilled onions on the side, waiting to be placed on top of the meat and pickle.

I don't know if it was the first approach to subliminal marketing, but because of one's proximity to the grill, by the time you left, your clothes were saturated with the delectable aroma of those little gems. Not only were you constantly reminded of the taste all the rest of the day, but everyone you sat next to or talked to would suddenly ask, "Hey, are you getting hungry?"

And what about hot dogs? Of course there were chili dogs, with or without sauerkraut, and dogs with just onions and piccalilli. But close to the intersection of North Avenue and Ogden was a wonderful place called Flukeys. After a hot summer's night ballgame, we would jump on the back of a truck, or if we had a lot of money—like 20 or 25 cents—we would splurge and take the old red streetcar for 3 cents.

Flukeys also started small. But if you offer quality and value, there is little need to advertise, and such was the case with Flukeys. He sold nothing but hot dogs and soda pop; that was the entire menu. But everything you could imagine was on the dog.

It all began with a super-fresh bun—like the White Castle, but of course it was a hot-dog bun—with sesame seeds on the top. The bun's lining was first artistically covered with mustard and then the plump, steamy wiener was dropped in. The hot dog was then trimmed with lettuce, tomato, piccalilli, chopped onion and a couple of hot peppers and topped off with a few French fries. Are you ready for this? A soda pop and hot dog were 10 cents—5 cents each if you only had a thirst or a hunger (or if you only had a nickel). My limit was three, but my big brother could handle five if he had the finances.

Even when the jingle in our pockets was only a tinkle, and at night when the trucks weren't running, we always had a second choice. Each night at dusk, the hot-dog vendors

with their converted baby buggies or custom pushcarts would light up gas lanterns and make their way to their regular street corners. They were all over—in front of Cubs' Park, whether a game was playing or not, on the corner of Sheffield and Belmont, next to the old Merry Gardens, across from the Vic movie house and on a hundred other street corners.

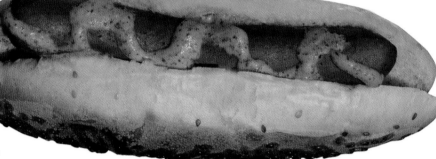

Photograph © 2009 by Emre Nicigil and www.sxc.hu

Each of these purveyors of the fine art of the hot dog had his individual touch for making a hot dog. And, like barbers and bartenders, they were patient listeners and imparters of great wisdom and philosophy, particularly after midnight when the rush was over. We knew such a person on Addison and Southport, a few blocks from St. Alphonsus Church. His name was Joe.

Joe was perhaps only in his early 40s, but in those days, a man of his age—an old man in our eyes—was to be respected and not interrupted. Joe came from Italy. The only difficulty in listening to him was that he had an accent so thick you could cut it. However, when we were kids, accents were commonplace and sort of fun to hear.

He talked about the Cubs, the weather, his kids and his hot dogs. But most of all, he talked about how much he loved America, and how very proud and how happy he would be when he became an American citizen.

I don't hear too many people talking like that today, even though I would guess there are a lot more Joes today than in those years. Joe took time to talk and to listen, and he also took his time to make what he honestly believed was the best hot dog in Chicago. I could never prove whether he did or didn't, but no one can say I didn't try. ❖

Soda Jerk

By Marlene Demetriou

The 1940s were the golden age of soda fountains and jukeboxes. My dad owned a confectionery/patent medicine store in Detroit, and after school I became a soda jerk. I jerked on syrup knobs and fizz-water knobs, and scooped ice cream till my wrist ached.

Our soda fountain had a marble-topped counter and padded swivel stools. Behind the counter was a sink, an array of syrup pumps and deep wells containing many flavors of ice cream. Behind them, mahogany cupboards lined the walls from floor to ceiling. On the shelves were glass soda, sundae and banana-split dishes and a glass straw holder. Apothecary jars filled with colored water brightened up the dark shelves on which they were stacked.

Soda jerks in the 1920s. Photo courtesy Duke University Libraries.

I was known for concocting the best sodas and milk shakes in the neighborhood. Making a soda required special talent. I maneuvered the fizz so as not to hit the ice cream and squirt my customer in the eye. I whipped up milk shakes and malts in a metal container with a blade that looked like an eggbeater.

My banana splits were works of art: three big scoops of ice cream and three flavors of topping, decorated with whipped cream, nuts and a cherry on top.

I made Boston coolers with Vernors ginger ale and brown cows with root beer. My frozen Lindies were one-of-a-kind, made by pouring pop into Dixie cups, freezing them and selling them to long lines of children for only 3 cents

a cup. At Christmastime, my dad played Santa Claus and entertained those long lines of children while I handed out candy.

In the back of our store was an elaborate jukebox where my after-school friends hung out, ate ice cream and played their favorite songs over and over. As the nickels went in and the 78-rpm platters were released, we'd watch the glowing colored lights. There were 24 songs on the jukebox, and we knew the words to every one of them. We loved it when the jukebox man came in and changed the records because he always gave us a free play.

I was fortunate to be able to read all the magazines that came in, especially the song and movie-star ones.

I learned a lot in that store in the late 1940s and early 1950s. I learned to communicate with people of all ages, to decorate store windows, and to purchase wholesale items. I took in utility bills and made money orders. Once a week, I walked a mile to catch a streetcar that took me to the nearest bank to deposit money. No one ever suspected that a young girl was carrying so much money in a paper bag.

Our old-fashioned soda fountain counter was one of the last of its kind. In the 1950s, when people started frequenting supermarkets to buy ice cream in bulk, the neighborhood soda-fountain hangouts began to fade away.

My years as a soda jerk were special. Every time I eat ice cream, it brings back a flood of good memories. ❖

Hamburgers by the Sack

By Mario DeMarco

Before McDonald's became the king of hamburgers, one fast-food company outdid all the others by selling hamburgers and other foods at fantastic prices. The name of this restaurant chain was White Castle, and as the name implies, their restaurants were constructed to look like small, white castles. We had a White Castle in my town on the corner of Main and Chandler streets, the two busiest streets in the city.

White Castles were so popular because they were spotlessly clean, accommodating, inexpensive (coffee sold for 5 cents a cup)—and their hamburgers were delicious.

On cold, snowy days when my brother and I made enough tips peddling newspapers, we would walk to the White Castle and enjoy a hamburger each. I can still remember the fine quality of the meat they used, and the hamburger bun had some "body" to it, unlike the soft, processed buns they serve today.

This outfit originated long before golden archways were ever dreamed of. The man responsible for the White Castle chain was Waldo "Billy" Ingram, who began promoting his business in Wichita, Kan., back in 1921. He began with a few hamburger stands, but it wasn't long before this new form of eating swept the country.

At one time, ground meat had been condemned as "leftover" meat. Ingram proved this belief wrong. Not only were his burgers healthy, but the price of 5

Above: Wow! What a deal! Facing page top: The compact White Castle restaurant in the author's town. Facing page bottom: When White Castle opened in the morning, everything was shining and spotless. The restaurants were inspected on a regular basis. Photos courtesy the author.

cents each (or three for a dime) was a deal! By the 1930s, White Castle had become the leading fast-food chain, and the hamburger had become America's food.

When war was declared on Dec. 8, 1941, White Castle faced labor shortages as well as food shortages. The first problem was soon solved when the company began hiring females; as for the second, White Castle began serving substitutes in place of some of the original menu items, which worked out just fine.

But by the end of the war, the chain had shrunk from 130 to only 87 restaurants, and in the following years, White Castle experienced other setbacks. However, the company came through with new ideas in marketing and expansion.

Numerous fast-food chains have come and gone, but White Castle has stood its ground for eight decades. And it still serves its fast food in more than 300 White Castle restaurants. ❖

Cokes Go Better at Granddaddy's

By Betty Rye Harvill

*S*ummers were hot and humid in Clarksville, Tenn., in the mid-1930s when my little brother, Jim, and I were young. Nobody we knew had air-conditioning; the grown-ups stayed up late and sat on their porches to take advantage of the cool night air. Some nights were so hot that we kids were allowed to stay up past our bedtimes and play out in the yard until things cooled off in the house.

Daddy's daddy had a barbershop on Franklin Street. We called him "Granddaddy" and so did most all our family. To others in town, though, and at church, where he was something of a pillar, he was simply "Mr. Rye." He was totally bald, short and stocky, and he was an impeccable dresser.

Jim loved to go down to Granddaddy's for his haircut. And if he wanted a Coke, all he had to do was ask, and Granddaddy would get one for him from the Coke machine in the shop. It always worked because Jim had been named after Granddaddy.

No bad language was allowed in Granddaddy's shop. Nothing off-color was said when Mr. Rye was around. He was a strict moralist and a strong churchman, and his customers respected him.

I hardly ever went to Granddaddy's shop—it wasn't a little girl's place. But Daddy, who worked in a furniture store up the street, took 5-year-old Jim there for his haircut every month or so. When Jim asked Granddaddy for a Coke, it bothered Daddy.

Photo © 2009 by Janice Tate

One evening after the monthly trip to Granddaddy's shop, Daddy took Jim aside and set him straight. "Jim, I don't want you asking Granddaddy for Cokes every time we get your hair cut," he said. "He's not rich, you know, and every one you drink costs him money. I mean it now. Don't ask him for any more Cokes. Understand?"

The next haircut day was a particularly hot one. Daddy took Jim down to Granddaddy's like always and sat him on the bench to wait his turn and listen to all the talk and watch the customers put nickels in the Coke machine. Jim was quiet for a long time, watching Granddaddy cut hair. But finally he called out, "Granddaddy?"

"Yes, Jim."

"Sure is a hot day."

"It sure is, Jim."

Jim was quiet again; then, "Granddaddy?"

"Yes?"

"A Coke sure would taste good on a hot day like this, wouldn't it?"

"Sure would, Jim. How about us having one?"

"OK by me, Granddaddy."

That was almost 60 years ago. Jim and I have grown kids now and grandkids too. Granddaddy has been gone a long time. So has Daddy.

Today, Jim lives in Southern California and is doing quite well. If you ask him, he'll probably say he still remembers Granddaddy's barbershop and sitting on that old bench on those hot summer days in Clarksville, drinking up Granddaddy's profits in Cokes. ❖

Freshly Burnt Coffee Beans

By John L. Patton

Growing up in the Cincinnati neighborhood of Fairmount during the 1950s, I had plenty of room to run and play, and plenty of fresh air—usually. Besides the normal sights and sounds, every once in a while there were also some interesting smells.

Across the street and a few doors down, Mouck's Bakery offered some sweet and tempting aromas. The smell of freshly baked bread was one I never tired of, but walking into their store in the morning was even better. Then their assortment of Danish pastries, yeast doughnuts and streusel were hard to resist.

It seemed that every store in Fairmount had its own set of odd or intriguing smells, and while they weren't always pleasant, they were distinctive. The dry cleaners often had a mild chemical stench, while the auto repair shop usually had a heavy oily scent coming from inside. Anne's Delicatessen, which was right next to the auto shop, had a mixture of tantalizing aromas, mostly from the meat counter and vegetable bin. Art's Candy Store, just across the street from Anne's, had some of the most inviting aromas of all.

Art's sold penny candy—which in those days really cost a penny—from wide, glass-fronted cases. Topping those cases were giant glass jars filled with more candy, as well as cookies, brownies and even pretzel rods. Art's was the first place most of us boys and girls ran whenever we had a few pennies burning holes in our pockets.

We would spend what seemed like forever trying to decide what to buy. We all had our favorites, but all those sweet and luscious aromas made choosing very difficult. I often bought Lunch Bars. They were only 3 cents each. Better-known brands, such as Hershey, cost 5 cents. Chocolate licorice was another favorite at two for a penny.

Another sweet-smelling store was Schmidt's Grocery, which was a block down the street and across from the Kenross Drugstore. They had installed the first creamy whip machine in the neighborhood, and the sweet, sugary aroma was almost as wonderful as the cool, velvety taste.

Kenross Drugstore, which had a soda fountain along the left side, had an odd mixture of smells, as the soda fountain competed with the medicine counter. We were able to ignore the medicine smell, especially when we were enjoying a sundae or banana split.

The most overwhelming aroma of all came from 3 miles away, from one of the many Kroger food-processing plants around Cincinnati. Kroger, a grocery giant even in the 1950s, was begun locally by Barney Kroger and produced a wide array of grocery items. Among other things, the plant near Eighth and State roasted coffee.

> *Most of the time, we enjoyed the bracing aroma of fresh-roasted coffee.*

Most of the time, we enjoyed the bracing aroma of fresh-roasted coffee. But every few weeks or so, we would have to suffer the overpowering stench of freshly burnt coffee beans. I can assure you that there are few smells as distracting as burnt coffee, especially when it lingers in the air for days. I'm still surprised that I eventually became a coffee drinker.

Nowadays I use instant coffee, since I only have an occasional cup. But I remember watching my mother use the machine that ground and then bagged coffee beans at the Kroger grocery on our street. The aroma of freshly ground beans was heavenly.

I don't know if groceries still have those coffee-grinding machines. If not, modern children are missing quite an experience. I also wonder if they have ever figured out how to stop burning coffee beans when they roast them. ❖

Lagniappe

By James D. Doggette Jr.

New Orleans is a cultural melting pot of everything from food to traditions. Because of its rich Creole heritage, one of the Crescent City's old-time customs was *lagniappe*. Lagniappe (pronounced LAN-yap) is a little something extra one receives from a merchant when one buys something from the store. Never was lagniappe more prevalent and plentiful in the "Big Easy" than in the late 1940s to mid-1950s. It is very rare today, but I still remember the day I first learned of it.

Summers at Grandma's, in the Lower Ninth Ward, were picturesque and wholesome—a literal Camelot for a kid growing up in that era. In this "kingdom" were a myriad of trees: climbing trees to vent a young boy's excess energy, incorporate his imagination and stimulate his curiosity. The old chinaberry tree that grew by the back of my grandparents' shotgun house was my favorite. I could find relief and release here in this lofty refuge, for sadness, gladness and tranquility.

> *She gave me a dollar bill and a grocery list, and then told me to run down to Mr. Louie's corner store.*

The topmost limbs branched out in a bucolic setting, with an 8-inch, circular, nest-type indentation at the base where I sometimes left my extra bubble gum, baseball cards and other treasures. My perch was just over the rooftops of the houses at that height, and I could see the neighborhood for blocks around from there. But no one could see me through the dense foliage as I sat there.

One day, at about 11 o'clock in the morning, I made my way up to that spot in my roost and sat there, dangling my legs while straddling a large branch. I was daydreaming of far-off, exotic places and adventures when my grandmother's voice interrupted my fantasy. "Yoo-hoo! Jayyy-meee!—Oh, Jamie!"

I looked down to see her calling me from the side door. I called back, "Yes, ma'am, I'm coming." I hurried down from the tree and ran to see what she wanted. She gave me a dollar bill and a grocery list, and then told me to run down to Mr. Louie's corner store to get some things for lunch.

I arrived at the store and entered by the screen door on the side. The cool breeze coming from the two big, black ceiling fans felt so good. I could feel it drying the sweat on my crew-cut head. Mr. Louie greeted me, "Ello, Jar-gee, *mon ami*." He asked me how I was doing and inquired about the rest of the family. Then, in his usual harmonic voice, he asked, "Now, what can I do for you?"

Facing page: A grocery store on a street corner in New Orleans in 1936.
Photo by Walker Evans courtesy the FSA/OWI Collection of the Library of Congress.

"One-half pound of luncheon meat, please."

He opened the deli cooler and took out the loaf of meat and put it on the slicer. I went about the rest of the list: one jar of mustard, one loaf of bread and a six-pack of root beer. I walked back to the counter with my groceries, and Mr. Louie was waiting there with the luncheon meat already wrapped up. "Is that all for you, Jar-gee, my boy?" he asked jovially.

I answered in the affirmative and he pressed buttons and pulled the crank handle on his cash register as he touched each item while mumbling to himself. Finally he hit a few more buttons, then pulled the lever twice. A bell rang and the cash drawer opened. "OK, Jar-gee boy, 88 cents for you," said Mr. Louie. I gave him the dollar bill and he gave me the change, and then put the items in a brown paper bag. I took the six-pack of root beer in one hand and wrapped my arm around the bag.

Mr. Louie told me to ask my grandmother for a bunch of parsley for him. I said that I would and bid him goodbye. When I got home, I told my grandma what Mr. Louie had asked for, and she went out to the victory garden along the fence. She picked two bunches of the herb and bound them with rubber bands. Then she told me to bring them down to the store and give them to Mr. Louie after we ate.

After lunch, I took the two bunches of parsley down to Mr. Louie's store and gave them to him. When he asked me how much Grandma wanted for them, I told him that she had said there was no charge. He quickly reached into one of the four large glass jars on the counter and laid out three big pieces of bubblegum. I looked at him with surprise and asked, "Whut-zat?"

"Man, that's *lagniappe*," he replied with a huge grin. ❖

Memory Lane Lunch

By Elizabeth Redman

A tuna-salad sandwich, a package of old-fashioned potato chips (the thin ones whose only flavorings were grease and salt) and a Coke—that was my favorite lunch at Flagstaff Pharmacy, across from the railroad station in Flagstaff, Ariz. The neighborhood drugstore was a special place in the 1940s and 1950s—not merely a section of a supermarket, or a huge, brightly lit variety store with toiletries and a medical section tucked in by the pharmacist's window, giving scant justification for the name "drugstore." Often called "the corner drugstore" by reason of its location, it was small by today's standards, and somewhat dark. But the lighting was adequate, and the customers and clerks looked healthier and less washed out than they do under today's brilliant illumination.

The drugstore in those days was a friendly, welcoming place. The person behind the lunch counter usually knew the customers, and if you were a regular, what you were likely to order.

> ### *If you were a regular, the person behind the lunch counter knew what you were likely to order.*

It was a place to meet an old friend or take a shopping break and have a Coke. If so inclined, you could splurge on a soda or a chocolate sundae. There was a penny scale outside, but it was positioned so that you didn't notice it until you were leaving—too late to interfere with the pleasure of indulgence!

The pharmacy was the most important department, of course, with the health and first-aid counter. But it was not the most interesting part of the store. That distinction was reserved for cosmetics and toiletries, easily located by a delightful fragrance.

Cosmetics were much simpler then, skin care being pretty well monopolized by creams. There were three basic kinds: vanishing, to wear during the day, under makeup; cleansing, to remove it; and night, to nourish the skin.

Powder and pancake makeup came in ivory, beige, suntan and rosy beige. Prominently displayed were the season's newest shades of lipstick and nail polish, such as Revlon's "Fire and Ice," keyed to the season's most fashionable colors. One line had a shade called "Natural." Though it was a most unnatural transparent orange in the tube, it turned a very pale pink on the lips. It made a good first lipstick for girls who had finally convinced their parents they were old enough to wear it.

Instead of blusher there was a choice of dry or cream rouge. The latter was a bit tricky to apply if you didn't want to look like a fugitive from Barnum and Bailey! Mascara and eyebrow pencils came in black and brown, and the mascara came in a little cake to be applied with a small brush. Brown, gray and blue, the basic eye-shadow shades, were supplemented by violet and green—the latter for redheads only.

Today's customers would be most familiar with the perfume section, including favorites such as Chanel No. 5, Muguet Des Bois, White Shoulders, and the most daringly exotic of all, Tabu.

The one we all remember, though, whether or not we ever wore it—or even liked it—was Evening in Paris, with its cobalt blue and silver packaging. Receiving an Evening in Paris gift set was a sure sign that you were becoming a young lady, your parents' opinion notwithstanding. And dressing table sets—mirror, brush and comb, with perhaps a powder jar—were so elegant and so nourishing to the feminine soul.

For discreetly powdering one's nose in public, there were compacts—enameled, jeweled and sophisticated metalwork designs. If one had an especially lovely compact, there was a lot of indiscreet "checking up"! And there were gift sets—dusting powder, bubble bath, cologne … it was a wonderful department!

The men had their own section with all the shaving necessities. Shaving, of course, was a different affair back then, far removed from modern disposable razors. On the contrary, it was generally accomplished with a razor whose blades could be changed as needed. The razors came in single- and double-edged styles, the single being slightly more useful as it also could be pressed into service scraping paint from windows, cutting cardboard and so forth.

A few older gentlemen still used straight razors, sharpening them on a long strap that hung in the bathroom, but these were fast falling from favor. They were far more dangerous—as evidenced by the styptic pencil that generally sat next to the razor in the medicine cabinet—and terrifying to look at; in fact, they were often employed as the weapon of choice in murder mysteries!

As aerosol cans had not yet been invented, the lather was produced with a brush and a round of soap in the bottom of a shaving mug, the latter now a collector's item. Some other gentlemen's toiletries are still familiar, particularly aftershave and cologne. Old Spice was the favorite among the men I knew—or perhaps, as it was a safe choice, it was just what they always received as gifts!

Other popular presents available at the drugstore were boxes of Russell Stover and Whitman's chocolates. The latter brand was packaged in a distinctive box with a map showing the way to the orange creams and other favorites. There were also boxes of chocolate-covered cherries and pastel creams—in the shapes of flowers, I think. They were so good, and especially appropriate at Easter and Mother's Day. Their special packaging was a real boon to gentlemen, as ready-made gift bows had not made their appearance.

The drugstore did carry gift wrap, ribbon and greeting cards, as well as stationery— always a safe gift for anyone, especially teachers, who rarely had to buy any for themselves. Nice notepaper was always a welcome gift too, as most communication was by mail. Telephone calls were generally reserved for emergencies or to announce the safe arrivals of babies and long-distance visits of family and friends.

On the way out the door, next to the pipes, tobacco and cigarettes, was a rack of paperbacks, a comic-book rack and the magazine section.

I always stopped to glance at the women's magazines. They seemed far less exhausting in those days; they focused on home arts, with occasional interviews with notable women and columns by such writers as Gladys Taber and Faith Baldwin. Some of the themes wouldn't make it past the door today, with features like "How to Help Your Husband Get Ahead."

Serials in the magazines by authors such as Agatha Christie and Rumer Godden were popular. The final chapter of one magazine serial always coincided with the first chapter of the next, safely hooking readers for a few more months!

Well-known illustrators did the covers, usually portraying a fashionable lady or perhaps a child. One of these magazines—*Ladies Home Journal*, I believe—employed top photographers and elegant models. Of all the "cover girls" featured, First Lady Eleanor Roosevelt was the one I remember most.

To my husband, a tuna-salad sandwich is just another lunch. To me, however, it's a ticket for a trip down memory lane! ❖

Soda Fountain Memories

By Dorothy Fairchild

In 1940 I worked at Walgreen's Drugstore on Main Street in Columbia, S.C. The store had a soda fountain with red-upholstered chrome stools along one side. At the end of the counter were three booths and two tables. I waited on the customers who were seated in the booths and at the tables. A young lad, Fred, worked as the "soda jerk" behind the counter.

I was fascinated by the way he made all the different concoctions our customers ordered. Being of an inquisitive nature, I soon learned to make all the different fountain orders too. Fred wasn't very ambitious, so he let me make the fountain orders. Soon I took over the fountain while continuing to serve the customers at the booths and tables as well.

One might wonder how a person learned to mix all those fountain drinks. Well, I'm here to tell you that Walgreen's had a book about 4 inches thick filled with formulas for everything that was served, and you had to make every fountain order "by the book"! To this day, I can tell you how to make a fountain Coke, milk shake, ice-cream soda or any other item sold there.

And the wonderful smell! I wish I could have bottled it! Sometimes I close my eyes and recall the sights, sounds and smells of drugstores back then.

Fred soon quit, and I was hired officially as his replacement. But when I asked to be paid the same wage Fred had earned, they turned me down. So I quit!

That's how it was in the Good Old Days. ❖

The author worked at this Walgreen's Drugstore soda fountain.
The poster over the back bar was part of a promotion during National Dairy Month.

Dime-Store Shopping

By Arlene Shovald

I think every kid's first shopping experience in Iron River, Mich., where I grew up, was at the J.J. Newberry store. The big sign above the entrance doors read "5–10 and 25 cents," and at that time, you really could purchase something for those modest amounts. J.J. Newberry's was one of several five-and-dimes that operated from the early 20th century. Woolworth's, Ben Franklin and Kresge's were others I remember, but we only had the Newberry store.

The company was founded by Joseph Josiah Newberry in Stroudsburg, Pa., in 1911. By the time he died in 1954, there were 475 stores. In 1961, near the end of the reign of the Newberry stores, there were 565 stores.

In the 1940s and 1950s, Friday night was shopping night in Iron River. Ours was a small mining community, and at that time, few women drove, so the late retail hours allowed the miners to bring their families into town to shop.

Red cinnamon hearts were in the candy case, and there were all kinds of valentines to choose from.

My dad, being a "Depression kid," had a sweet tooth like you wouldn't believe. (Candy had been a rare treat when he was growing up.) Consequently, one of the first stops on Friday night was the candy counter at the Newberry store. The smell of fresh roasted peanuts and cashews combined with the sweet scents of candy to create an indescribable aroma that was uniquely Newberry store.

The candy was displayed in bins with glass fronts. Some of my dad's favorites were orange marshmallow circus peanuts (they tasted kind of like bananas) and root beer barrels. The girl behind the counter would scoop up what we wanted, weigh it and pour it into a white sack. Then we'd walk around the store, nibbling on the candies while we did our shopping.

Once, when I was in grade school, I went to the Newberry store by myself during lunch hour and saw that the hard Christmas candy, which my dad loved, was marked on sale for "7 cents a lb." When I got off the school bus, I hurried home and proudly announced that candy was on sale for "7 cents a lib" at the Newberry store. I was teased about that forever! I didn't know that "lb." was an abbreviation for "pound"!

The Newberry store was the place to go for school supplies too. There was always a colorful array of tablets, crayons and pencil boxes that held a protractor that no one ever used.

In the early grades, I chose a Big Chief tablet and pencils. I felt very grown-up when I graduated to a three-ring notebook and notebook paper.

The Newberry store was also the place to go for holidays. The highlight of my year was when the Halloween masks were displayed across from the candy counter. I would stand on tiptoe, straining to see the masks. I must have spent an hour making up my mind.

The masks back then were all made of something that looked like heavily starched cheesecloth. We needed new masks every year because the moisture from our breath caused them to go limp by the end of Halloween night.

Christmas at the dime store was nearly as exciting as Halloween. I saved all year to buy presents. I usually ended up with $10 or $15 by Thanksgiving.

The Newberry store was, of course, the first—and often the only—stop. Radio Girl perfume was 10 cents plus 2 cents luxury tax. Blue Waltz was a bit pricier at 15 cents plus the luxury tax. They also had bottles of cologne that were shaped like little oil lamps, complete with plastic shades. They were really expensive at 39 cents! My mother still has some of those little oil-lamp perfume containers I bought her.

The dime store was the place to go for Valentine's Day too. Red cinnamon hearts and conversation hearts were in the candy case, and there were all kinds of valentines to choose from. I liked the ones with a sucker attached that said something like "Sweets for the sweet." But whether I got those depended on how many kids were in my class that year; they were the most expensive valentines in the store.

The Newberry store was great for Easter shopping as well. Rows and rows of Easter baskets wrapped in cellophane and tied with bows enticed the younger set, and there were plenty of chocolate eggs and bunnies.

After graduating from high school in 1958, I took a job at the Newberry store and got to write names in icing on chocolate eggs and bunnies. That year we also sold live chickens and ducks tinted in pastel colors. Most of them were sold by Easter, but a few sickly ones remained. Rather than see them "executed," I took several home to nurse back to health. Eventually those cuddly little puffs of pastel turned into real birds with feathers, and we ended up giving them to a farmer.

By 1959, I was married, and the 5-, 10- and 25-cent price tags at the Newberry store had gone by the wayside. Most were $1 and up. I worked in the fabric and drapery department where you could buy a set of plastic drapes that smelled strongly of some kind of chemical for $1. Fabric began at about 25 cents a yard, and when I was expecting our first baby, I bought enough to sew all my maternity clothes and a layette for the baby.

By the time I was eight months pregnant, though, it was nicely "suggested" that I leave my job. Women "in my condition" in the workplace were frowned on in those days. That ended my working career for the next 11 years. With four babies in five years, I was up to my eyeballs in work at home!

I don't know when the Newberry store closed in Iron River, Mich., but I have no memories of taking my own children there. The building where it once stood is now occupied by another store. But every time I visit there, I can still see that candy counter where Christmas candy was on sale for "7 cents a lib" and the Halloween masks on the other side of the aisle. My favorite dime store may be gone, but it certainly isn't forgotten. ❖

The author, age 9, with her new Christmas doll in 1949. It came to her from Santa Claus by way of the J.J. Newberry Store, where she spotted the doll on the shelves in early December. She was surprised that Santa found exactly the right one. It was her last doll.

Department Store Tubes

By John Dinan

I made my first trip to a large downtown department store very reluctantly. Hanging on to my mother's hand while she traversed the many floors and aisles was torture beyond belief for a 6-year-old. There was nothing there for a kid, except maybe the elevator, which was all too short-lived.

But things picked up when it came time for my mother to pay for her purchases. The salesman, writing up the sale and accepting my mother's cash (these were pre-credit-card days), placed the cash and sales slip in a round canister with brass ends and placed the mysterious object in a tube, sending it whistling off through an overhead maze of tubes.

Thoughts of Buck Rogers and Flash Gordon filled my mind. This was like space travel! Did that rocket go to some strange port?

As I sat there waiting with my mother, I heard the rocket swoosh through the tubes overhead, banging in the turns, as it made its return voyage. The salesman opened the tube and handed my mother her change and the sales slip.

It may have been a matter-of-fact transaction for the two of them, but this pneumatic voyage was the stuff of imagination for me. Thoughts of humans (me, specifically) traveling through space in just such a system filled my head on the way home. These thoughts fired my imagination for weeks, and to tell the truth, I have never fully gotten over the beauty and the efficiency of this system.

So it came as no surprise when I read in the local paper that the Boston Public Library uses—guess what? "To send a book request back to the stacks, a clerk places a slip of paper into a rounded canister and sends the message to the correct destination through a highway of pneumatic tubes. The curator, Scot Cornwall, says the same thing could be accomplished with a network of computer terminals, printers and the right software, but computers cost money, require training and can be awfully temperamental."

Cornwall gives his blessing to the tubes, saying they are "quick and generally foolproof." He added, "I am extremely happy with them."

There's something else about tubes. They're a pleasure to operate, are fun to watch, and have a capacity for exciting one's imagination. I've never had that experience with a computer! ❖

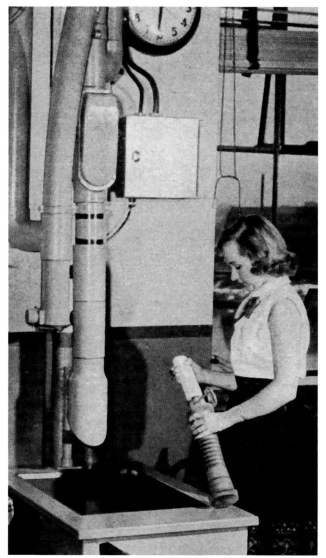

A demonstration of how pneumatic tubes worked was featured in the December 1951 issue of Popular Science *magazine.*

Free Bubble Gum

By Mary M. Chase

The Depression in Oklahoma City left me with many recollections, both bad and good. But this childhood memory is a treasured keepsake. My neighbor Ethel and I often played dress-up in our mothers' worn-out dresses—and I mean worn out. They were threadbare, but they were treasures to us, along with their crushed, faded hats, gloves, high heels and limp black purses. When we donned all this gear, we considered ourselves smashingly stylish, ready for a tea party or a shopping spree.

On this day, we decided to go shopping. My blue pillbox hat topped my head, with its veil pinned down over each ear. Ethel wore her sister's yellow, floppy, wide-brimmed hat that almost covered her blond Shirley Temple curls. With our dresses girded up so as not to drag, we clomped off the porch in our heels, each dangling a purse from an arm. We were ready.

With three pennies between us, we decided to make Higbee's Grocery around the corner our first stop. We planned to buy two pieces of candy for a penny and two pieces of bubble gum with the remaining 2 cents.

When we finally reached the store, we clambered up the two steps and through the double screened doors adorned with ads: "Colonial is Good Bread." And it *was* good bread, especially with Grandma's blackberry jelly.

Once inside, we browsed and talked about our make-believe purchases. We felt everything in the barrels, touched anything handy, read all the signs we could and made plans for our next stop. Mr. Higbee and a salesman stood nearby, talking, and the salesman's bag sat open near his feet.

Ethel's shoe caught in the hem of her dress and she tripped backward over the salesman's bag. Ethel, her shoes and purse flipped through the air after bumping the salesman. He hit a small barrel of peanuts, sending them scattering to the four winds. All I could see was the barrel spinning 'round and 'round, scattering peanuts everywhere. Ethel sprawled on the floor amidst the peanuts, hat and glasses cocked off to one side, her myopic little eyes going crazy.

I don't think Mr. Higbee or I ever moved. It happened so quickly. The salesman crunched over the peanuts to pick up "the little lady," as he called her. He lifted her across the peanuts and helped her straighten her hat and glasses.

The Sweetest Spot in Town by John Slobodnik
© House of White Birches nostalgia archives

After we all had regained our composure, and Ethel got her shoes back on and retrieved her purse, Mr. Higbee gave us each a piece of bubble gum and kindly suggested that we go elsewhere to do our shopping. He didn't even ask us to help pick up the peanuts. ❖

Ups and Downs

By Helen Patton Gray

At age 8, back in 1938, I was fascinated by elevators, especially the one in the old Altman Building in downtown Kansas City, Mo., where my father worked. On several occasions, Dad took me along to help mail advertising materials. It was fun to sit at his desk, folding brochures, stuffing envelopes, playing office. However, the best part of the day was riding the elevator to and from the second floor. I watched people come and go, stepping onto the elevator after merely pressing a button to call for it. Then, after closing a polished-brass folding gate, the operator magically pushed another button on the panel inside, and the little room moved up and down. I was amazed!

We always got off on the second floor, although there were four or five floors above with all sorts of business offices and shops. In 1938, nobody went to malls. There were none.

My mother came with Dad and me one day to buy a hat at a millinery store in the building. She took me along to the fifth floor. It was a treat to go up higher so I could ride longer and see more of the building.

We walked down the terrazzo-floored hallway to the entrance of the hat store, which featured a huge display of felt hats with fancy plumage, bows and streamers as well as shiny gold pins like the ones movie stars wore. Some hats were very plain with no trim, just plain black with floppy wide brims. I thought those were ugly—nothing my mother would select.

Then, as Mom sat down at a dressing table, the shop lady slipped one of those ugly, plain, felt numbers on her head. I chuckled quietly; the hat looked strange, like something a hobo would wear. Turning my head, I gazed around the shop, just to keep from laughing out loud. I knew that would be rude and embarrass Mom.

Finally the shop lady picked up some pretty chiffon fabric and a jeweled pin and placed it on the ugly hat. She pinned the fabric in several places and like magic, the bare felt hat was transformed into a lovely chapeau. My eyes widened; now the hat looked like something Mom or a movie star would wear!

The shop lady said she would have the hat completed in a few days, and Mom could come back for a final fitting. Then we left the shop to take another elevator ride. This time we stopped on the third floor, where there was a small restaurant. Mom let me choose what I wanted, so I had chocolate ice cream topped with whipped cream and a cherry. Then we took the elevator down to the first floor and left the Altman Building to do some more shopping in downtown department stores.

The best part of the day was riding the elevator to and from the second floor.

As we shopped, there were more elevator rides up and down, plus an escalator in one of the stores. I thought it was a treat to be transported for free, unlike the streetcars and buses, which cost 10 cents each way. Finally we finished our shopping and left for home.

A few years later, escalators replaced most of the elevators, and most of the remaining elevators were replaced by newer models. The newer elevators were faster, but not as much fun. There were no brass gates, no operators. Passengers had to be their own operators, pushing the buttons and watching the lights above the door to be sure they got off at the right floor.

Today, airports have moving sidewalks. Some have subways that move hundreds of people from one concourse to another as they stand, packed in like sardines.

While they are more efficient, there's something to be said for the elevators of the 1930s and 1940s, which had an operator on board who greeted you and asked "Floor, please?" ❖

Street Vendors

By Bill Connell

As I sit here thinking of all the fast ways we live today, I feel a pang of sorrow about the things that are no more. Let's think back to our younger days and drift off to the 1930s. I remember something today's young folks will never know about—the street vendors. What joy they used to bring to us kids—and to our elders also.

Some of the more advanced vendors had horses pulling their carts. The scrap-and-paper man had a two-horse wagon and collected scrap iron and used newspapers. Now, mind you, the papers had to be completely dry, or he refused to take them. He said he paid out more money if they were wet.

He would come into our basement and go to a box next to Dad's coal bin where we kept our pile of used papers. He carried a net bag and would put the papers he selected in it, then weigh them with a hand scale. It was my job to see they were weighed correctly, although I never did actually see the scale. After he completed his weighing, we were paid a few pennies per pound, and off they went. (By the way, a boy might make some candy money by searching the neighborhood for newspapers to add to the pile.)

> *Some of the more advanced vendors had horses pulling their carts.*

Two horses also pulled the ice wagon. Oh, the joys that one brought! Mom would send me downstairs to tell the iceman we wanted 15 or 20 cents' worth of ice. He would proceed to cut the ice and carry it up three flights of stairs and put it in the bottom of the icebox. We always managed to get a piece of sweet-tasting ice from him.

Do you remember the fruit-and-vegetable man? He only had one horse pulling his wagon; I guess the produce was not that heavy. There was always a chance of getting something from him.

He was one of the nicer people, and he gave bruised fruit and vegetables to the children when the parent made a purchase. Of course, if we followed him down the street, there was always the chance that something would fall off the wagon. And there were always boys who ran up from behind to snatch a grape or two. But I never was involved in anything like that.

Those with the horse-drawn wagons were the more modern vendors. But the ones I liked most were the ones with pushcarts. They seemed to be the hardest workers of all. Didn't matter what the weather was; most were out there, selling. The sharpening man pushed a handcart down the street. He had a hard time in wet, snowy weather. I liked to watch him because

Facing page: Photo courtesy House of White Birches nostalgia archives

he made sparks while he worked. He pumped the grinding stone by a pedal, and boy, did sparks fly when metal touched stone! He sharpened any item we brought to him, and when he was finished, it was usually better than new. But only once do I remember Dad using him.

It was for a pair of scissors Mom used for sewing. She was always so touchy about those scissors. I think poor Dad was afraid to sharpen them himself for fear of making a mistake. But he told me it was because he did not have the correct stone for the job. Well, the sharpening man got the job, and Mom was happy, and Dad was happy, so it worked out all right.

Another pushcart man was the fish vendor. I never liked to be near him. Boy, did his cart

smell! But Dad could hardly wait for him to arrive. Once a month, Dad would go down and buy a platter of shrimp and clams. He was the happiest person that night, listening to the radio and eating his monthly catch.

One of my favorites was the Italian-ice man. This fellow could have been voted most popular in the entire neighborhood. He sold flavored, colored ice in tiny cardboard cups. I can taste it now! He piled it over the top of the little cup. By the time I was finished, the cup was crushed from squeezing it, and I was generally covered with colored ice. But that was the only way to eat it.

We could not afford to get his ice every day, but Mom tried to let me have ice once a week. On ice day, I was at the doorway of the apartment, just waiting. No way was he going to get past me! That had happened once, and I never wanted it to happen again.

I have saved the very best for last. I know you will question whether or not he was really a vendor, but you must remember, I was born a boy. This one was the most exciting: the two-horse garbage wagon.

Oh, go ahead and laugh! But you have no idea of the memories that one conjures up. I believe these were by far the smartest people in the world. The collectors always let boys throw the garbage up and into the wagon. Meanwhile, they stood there and coached us.

The fun we had just tossing the garbage into a wagon is a mystery to me. As I think back, I have to smile at all the free work I must have done for the garbage collectors. But then, as payment, we were allowed to ride the back platform of the wagon. It went very slowly and a very short distance, so it was safe.

Now I look out and see one big truck with one garbage collector going down the street. He picks up the large garbage cans with a big hook. Sadly, the small boys in the neighborhood don't even give him a glance. They will never know the joy of waiting for one of the street vendors to come down the road.

I think I was a lucky boy back then to have seen and been a part of the street vendors. I have a wealth of memories and many, many smiles about this part of the Good Old Days! ❖

Facing page: Photo courtesy FSA/OWI Collection, Library of Congress

Babe's Drugstore

By Jacquelyn Coleman Williams

When I was a little girl growing up in Steubenville, Ohio, my Grandma Julia Coleman liked to take me with her to Babe's Drugstore. My Grandma Julia lived at Pleasant Heights and Lawson Avenue. Babe's Drugstore, a small, friendly neighborhood pharmacy, was a half-block from Grandma's house, also on Lawson Avenue.

On hot, sultry summer afternoons, my grandma would sometimes say, "Let's go to Babe's Drugstore and get an ice-cream cone." We'd walk the half-block to Babe's, and when we opened the door, a little bell jangled to announce us.

Inside, the wonderful, delicious smell of vanilla filled our senses. Babe's Drugstore always smelled like vanilla.

Babe stood in the back of the drugstore and called out a hearty greeting. He was a big man, nearly bald, and he always wore his white pharmacist's coat.

While Grandma looked over the magazines on the large rack, I could pick out a 10-cent Donald Duck comic book. Then we asked for our vanilla ice-cream cones, a refreshing treat on a hot summer afternoon.

When we left Babe's Drugstore, savoring our ice-cream cones, the little bell above the door jangled a brief goodbye.

Babe's Drugstore is no longer there; it has been replaced by a flower shop. Yet even today, many years later and more than 2,000 miles away, every time I use vanilla for baking or smell that delicious aroma, I picture Babe's Drugstore with the smiling Babe dressed in his neat, white coat, and I remember that wonderful smell of vanilla that always greeted us as we entered. ❖

The Lost Umbrella

By Dorothy Rice

*I*t was 1952 and I was 7 years old. I lived in Lynchburg, Va., with my mom, dad, older brother and two younger brothers. Every two weeks, Mom and I would go get groceries at a store called the Dutch Market.

We would gather all of our groceries in a basket and pay for them. Then we would leave them there, and the store would deliver them that evening in a big banana box.

Before two weeks were up, Mom would send me to Governors Store, about 20 minutes away. There I would buy milk, bread, lunch meat and so on to tide us over until we could go get groceries again.

One day when Mom sent me to Governors, it was cloudy, so she told me to take our umbrella. She always told me to take real good care of it, as it was the only one we had. Times were tough back then; you couldn't afford a lot. Someone had given us that umbrella. Anyway, I went on to the store.

I was walking home with my bag of milk, bread, lunch meat and a few other items. What I thought was a storm became a hurricane! I never saw so much rain and wind. I really was scared.

At the top of the street that led to my house, all of a sudden, the grocery bag busted! All of the groceries were going down the street in a big stream of water.

And, to everything off, my umbrella was blown away.

I was standing there crying when our neighbor pulled up. He got out of his car and helped me gather what groceries he could salvage. I asked him to look for the umbrella, but he couldn't find it.

When we got to our house, my older brother, Pete, was getting ready to go looking for me. Our neighbor told Mom how he had found me crying.

After Mom helped me dry off and got me settled down, she asked me where the umbrella was. I was too scared to tell her that the wind had blown it out of my hands, so I told her a dog stole it. My brother asked what color the dog was.

I answered that it was a brown dog with a white tail. He and Mom laughed. My brother said that there was no such color of dog in the neighborhood. Then I admitted that I had been afraid to tell her that it had blown away.

"We are just glad you are OK," Mom said. "Don't worry about the umbrella."

When my brother and I get together, we talk about that time. We have fond memories of the Good Old Days. When it rains and I put my umbrella up, I often think about that day. ❖